Terrorism: A Very Short Introduction

Very Short Introductions available now:

ACCOUNTING Christopher Nobes
ADVERTISING Winston Fletcher
AFRICAN AMERICAN RELIGION
    Eddie S. Glaude Jr
AFRICAN HISTORY
    John Parker and Richard Rathbone
AFRICAN RELIGIONS Jacob K. Olupona
AGNOSTICISM Robin Le Poidevin
AGRICULTURE Paul Brassley and
    Richard Soffe
ALEXANDER THE GREAT Hugh Bowden
ALGEBRA Peter M. Higgins
AMERICAN HISTORY Paul S. Boyer
AMERICAN IMMIGRATION
    David A. Gerber
AMERICAN LEGAL HISTORY
    G. Edward White
AMERICAN POLITICAL HISTORY
    Donald Critchlow
AMERICAN POLITICAL PARTIES AND
    ELECTIONS L. Sandy Maisel
AMERICAN POLITICS Richard M. Valelly
THE AMERICAN PRESIDENCY
    Charles O. Jones
THE AMERICAN REVOLUTION
    Robert J. Allison
AMERICAN SLAVERY
    Heather Andrea Williams
THE AMERICAN WEST Stephen Aron
AMERICAN WOMEN'S HISTORY
    Susan Ware
ANAESTHESIA Aidan O'Donnell
ANARCHISM Colin Ward
ANCIENT ASSYRIA Karen Radner
ANCIENT EGYPT Ian Shaw
ANCIENT EGYPTIAN ART AND
    ARCHITECTURE Christina Riggs
ANCIENT GREECE Paul Cartledge
THE ANCIENT NEAR EAST
    Amanda H. Podany
ANCIENT PHILOSOPHY Julia Annas
ANCIENT WARFARE Harry Sidebottom
ANGELS David Albert Jones
ANGLICANISM Mark Chapman
THE ANGLO-SAXON AGE John Blair
THE ANIMAL KINGDOM Peter Holland
ANIMAL RIGHTS David DeGrazia
THE ANTARCTIC Klaus Dodds
ANTISEMITISM Steven Beller
ANXIETY Daniel Freeman and
    Jason Freeman
THE APOCRYPHAL GOSPELS Paul Foster
ARCHAEOLOGY Paul Bahn
ARCHITECTURE Andrew Ballantyne
ARISTOCRACY William Doyle
ARISTOTLE Jonathan Barnes

ART HISTORY Dana Arnold
ART THEORY Cynthia Freeland
ASTROBIOLOGY David C. Catling
ASTROPHYSICS James Binney
ATHEISM Julian Baggini
AUGUSTINE Henry Chadwick
AUSTRALIA Kenneth Morgan
AUTISM Uta Frith
THE AVANT GARDE David Cottington
THE AZTECS David Carrasco
BACTERIA Sebastian G. B. Amyes
BARTHES Jonathan Culler
THE BEATS David Sterritt
BEAUTY Roger Scruton
BESTSELLERS John Sutherland
THE BIBLE John Riches
BIBLICAL ARCHAEOLOGY Eric H. Cline
BIOGRAPHY Hermione Lee
BLACK HOLES Katherine Blundell
THE BLUES Elijah Wald
THE BODY Chris Shilling
THE BOOK OF MORMON Terryl Givens
BORDERS Alexander C. Diener and
    Joshua Hagen
THE BRAIN Michael O'Shea
BRICS Andrew F. Cooper
THE BRITISH CONSTITUTION
    Martin Loughlin
THE BRITISH EMPIRE Ashley Jackson
BRITISH POLITICS Anthony Wright
BUDDHA Michael Carrithers
BUDDHISM Damien Keown
BUDDHIST ETHICS Damien Keown
BYZANTIUM Peter Sarris
CANCER Nicholas James
CAPITALISM James Fulcher
CATHOLICISM Gerald O'Collins
CAUSATION Stephen Mumford and
    Rani Lill Anjum
THE CELL Terence Allen and Graham Cowling
THE CELTS Barry Cunliffe
CHAOS Leonard Smith
CHEMISTRY Peter Atkins
CHILD PSYCHOLOGY Usha Goswami
CHILDREN'S LITERATURE
    Kimberley Reynolds
CHINESE LITERATURE Sabina Knight
CHOICE THEORY Michael Allingham
CHRISTIAN ART Beth Williamson
CHRISTIAN ETHICS D. Stephen Long
CHRISTIANITY Linda Woodhead
CITIZENSHIP Richard Bellamy
CIVIL ENGINEERING David Muir Wood
CLASSICAL LITERATURE William Allan
CLASSICAL MYTHOLOGY Helen Morales
CLASSICS Mary Beard and John Henderson

Charles Townshend

TERRORISM

A Very Short Introduction

OXFORD

UNIVERSITY PRESS

Great Clarendon Street, Oxford OX2 6DP

Oxford University Press is a department of the University of Oxford.
It furthers the University's objective of excellence in research, scholarship,
and education by publishing worldwide in

Oxford New York

Auckland Cape Town Dar es Salaam Hong Kong Karachi
Kuala Lumpur Madrid Melbourne Mexico City Nairobi
New Delhi Shanghai Taipei Toronto

With offices in

Argentina Austria Brazil Chile Czech Republic France Greece
Guatemala Hungary Italy Japan Poland Portugal Singapore
South Korea Switzerland Thailand Turkey Ukraine Vietnam

Oxford is a registered trade mark of Oxford University Press
in the UK and in certain other countries

Published in the United States
by Oxford University Press Inc., New York

© Charles Townshend 2011

First edition published 2002
This edition published 2011

British Library Cataloguing in Publication Data

Data available

Library of Congress Cataloging in Publication Data

Data available

Typeset by SPI Publisher Services, Pondicherry, India
Printed in Great Britain on acid-free paper by
Ashford Colour Press Ltd, Gosport, Hampshire

ISBN 978-0-19-960394-7

7 9 10 8 6

Contents

List of illustrations

Chapter 1
The trouble with terrorism

> An attempt upon a crowned head or a president is
> sensational enough in a way, but not so much as it used to be.
> It has entered into the general conception of the existence of
> all chiefs of state . . . Now let us take an outrage upon – say – a
> church. Horrible enough at first sight no doubt, and yet not
> so effective as a person of ordinary mind might think. No
> matter how revolutionary and anarchist in inception, there
> would be fools enough to give such an outrage the character
> of a religious manifestation. And that would detract from the
> especial alarming significance we wish to give to the act . . .
> You can't count upon their emotions either of pity or fear for
> very long. A bomb outrage to have any influence on public
> opinion must go beyond the intention of vengeance or
> terrorism. It must be purely destructive.
>
> Joseph Conrad, *The Secret Agent* (1907)

Terrorism upsets people. It does so deliberately. That is its point,
and that is why it has engrossed so much of our attention in the
early years of the 21st century. Insecurity can take many forms, but
nothing else plays quite so sharply on our sense of vulnerability.
After 9/11, we found ourselves in an apparently open-ended and
permanent state of emergency, a 'war against terror', whose
ramifications are as inscrutable as terrorism itself. Terrorism is
never easy to understand, and least of all in the aftermath of a

terrorist attack. When society feels under threat, attempts at rational analysis are often openly resisted as giving aid and comfort to, or even sympathizing with, the enemy. Yet without such analysis, combating terrorism seems a baffling contest against an indefinite threat. Although terrorism can sometimes look rational, more often it seems to go straight off the chart of 'common sense' – to be not only unjustifiable, but atrocious, mad, or 'mindless'.

Something about terrorism makes its threat inflate, genie-like, way beyond its actual physical scale. Images of terrorism, in newspaper cartoons or on the covers of the avalanche of books on the subject published over the last generation, typically set giant weapons against shrunken targets. Before 9/11 at least, most writers on terrorism recognized that the physical threat posed by terrorism was dwarfed by other more everyday dangers. But even then, ordinary people, or their political representatives, showed little inclination to minimize the threat, or put it in perspective. Often urged on by a mass media that magnified the public danger, politicians rushed to answer the implicit or explicit call for protective action. That action was, however, usually inconsistent and episodic. 9/11 called for more than this.

Terrorism shot to the top of the political agenda, and from then on it would be hard to contend that the damage it could cause was comparatively trivial, or even – a familiar argument – that its psychological effect was out of proportion to its physical effect. New York saw damage that looked like a wartime air raid. Although the casualty list mercifully shrank from a potential 50,000 to less than 4,000, the vision of mass destruction, previously restricted to the kind of weapons possessed by only a handful of major powers, had appeared. The attack was deadlier, in terms of fatalities in a single day, than the bloodiest battles of the American Civil War. But unlike in war, the destruction – however awesome – was isolated. No invading armies appeared. If this was war, it was far from the familiar, almost comforting, conventions of traditional warfare. As the dust settled, literally and figuratively, on Ground Zero, most of the questions that had always formed the puzzle of terrorism remained. If anything, the indefinite reach of President Bush's 'war against terror' underlined more sharply than ever the need for some definition – or compartmentalization – of this manipulable term.

The problem of definition

Both political and academic efforts to get to grips with terrorism have repeatedly been hung up on the issue of definition, of distinguishing terrorism from criminal violence or military action. Most writers have no trouble compiling a list of legal or other definitions running into dozens – and then adding their own to it. One well-known survey opens with a whole chapter on the issue; another managed to amass over a hundred definitions before concluding that the search for an 'adequate' definition was still on. Why the difficulty? In a word, it is labelling, because 'terrorist' is a description that has almost never been voluntarily adopted by any individual or group. It is applied to them by others, first and foremost by the governments of the states they attack. States have not been slow to brand violent opponents with this title, with its clear implications of inhumanity, criminality, and – perhaps most crucially – lack of real political support. Equally, states find it quite easy to produce definitions of terrorism. The USA, for instance, defines it as 'the calculated use or threat of violence to inculcate fear, intended to coerce or intimidate governments or societies'; the UK as 'the use or threat, for the purpose of advancing a political, religious, or ideological course of action, of serious violence against any person or property'.

Having done this, though, they tend to find it harder to specify the behaviour thus indicted; there is no specifically 'terrorist' action that is not already a crime under the ordinary law. Instead, they label certain organizations as 'terrorist' and make membership of them an offence, and they draw up schedules of proscibed offences such as possession of explosives or taking hostages. Britain has come up with an offence called 'preparation of an act of terrorism', which seems to echo the notorious conspiracy laws of earlier times. Ultimately, terrorism appears to be defined by intention rather than behaviour.

The problem here is that state definitions simply assume that the use of violence by 'subnational groups' (as the US Department of State's definition has it) is automatically illegal. In the state's view, only the state has the right to use force – it has, as academics tend to say, a monopoly on the legitimate use of violence. But outsiders may wonder whether all use of violence by non-state actors is equally unjustifiable, even if it is formally illegal. The very first revolutionary terrorists in the modern sense, as we shall see in Chapter 4, believed themselves justified in opposing with violence a repressive regime in which no freedom of political expression or organization was permitted. And, crucially, many foreign critics of Tsarist Russia – governments included – agreed with them. (This has continued to be the case, as when Syria publicly, and embarrassingly refused to endorse the British and American insistence that Arab armed actions against Israel are part of a single global phenomenon of terrorism.) These differences of perspective gave rise to the notorious adage that 'one person's terrorist is another's freedom fighter'. This relativism is central to the impossibility of finding an uncontentious definition of terrorism.

Some writers have suggested that instead of pursuing the will-o'-the-wisp of precise definition (one specialist has called terrorism 'a box with a false bottom') it would make more sense to construct a typology of the kinds of actions that are generally seen as 'terrorist'. It is certainly the case that many kinds of action repeatedly used by terrorist groups – assassination, kidnapping, hijacking – are seldom if ever used in conventional military conflicts; they do seem to signal a special type of violence. But any such list soon peters out: too many terrorist actions duplicate either military or criminal acts. In any case, it is, in the end, not so

1. The attackers of New York's World Trade Center, on 11 September 2001, created an unparalleled shock effect, but signally failed to communicate their motivation and intention to their victims

much the actions themselves that are characteristic of terrorism, as their intended political function. 'Terror is simply a tactic, a method of random violence', as the political scientist Sunil Khilnani says, 'as likely to be used by a deranged individual as by a state. But *terrorism* is a distinctive form of modern political agency, intended to threaten the ability of a state to ensure the security of its members' – and thus its claim to legitimacy. To get closer to a definition of terrorism we need to unpick its political logic. For the core of nearly all definitions of terrorism – the use of violence for political ends – is too similar to the definition of war to be of much use.

Terrorism and war

Clearly war and terror are intimately related. It is hard to imagine a war that did not generate extreme fear amongst many people, and sometimes this is more than a by-product of violence – it is a primary objective. Historically, the sacking of captured cities was definitely intended to intimidate the inhabitants of other fortified positions (whether combatants or noncombatants). More recently, the development of strategic air bombing, though it had a strictly military rationale – to avoid the costly stalemate of trench warfare as experienced in the First World War – was based on a psychological theory: the belief that it could undermine the morale of the enemy population. In the words of one of its founding fathers, Lord Trenchard, in a bombing duel the enemy 'would squeal before we did'. In the event, this belief proved to be, if not false, certainly exaggerated, so the scale of destruction required to implement it after 1940 became vastly greater than had previously been imagined (or possible).

By the time of the gigantic raids on Hamburg and Dresden, the description of the RAF's operations as terror bombing was not merely the rhetoric of Goebbels's propaganda ministry: this was undeniably a deliberate attack on noncombatants. Even so, the dreams of the apostles of air power – the Wellsian nightmares of the civilians – did not become reality. The Second World War was not won by bombing. It has proved difficult to determine precisely the role it played – whether 'decisive' or not – but it was ultimately auxiliary to the kind of traditional military action so despised by airmen. And neither has any subsequent war been won by bombing alone. In war, fear may be a potent weapon, but it is not an omnipotent one.

One way of distinguishing war from terrorism might be to say that war is what states do, terrorism is the recourse of those too weak to oppose states openly. But this misses the point that the weak may adopt a strategy of resistance that does not require terror. Guerrilla warfare, however 'unconventional' by regular military criteria, operates by normal military logic. Guerrilla fighters engage the state's armed forces, on however small a physical scale, and however protracted or episodic a timescale, and thus fulfil Clausewitz's requirement that war be 'the collision of two living forces', not 'the action of a living force upon a lifeless mass'. In other words, the defining process of war is combat.

The essence of terrorism, by contrast, is surely the negation of combat. Terrorist targets are attacked in a way that inhibits (or better prohibits) self-defence. But, of course, what marks terrorism out in the public mind is its readiness to attack not just selected but also random targets; in the indiscriminate bombing of a street market, a store, or a bar, we see a deliberate flouting of the international law of war, and a refusal to accept as binding the prevailing moral distinctions – between belligerents and neutrals, combatants and noncombatants, legitimate and illegitimate targets. So the vital part of the US definition is the 'noncombatant targets' against whom violence is 'perpetrated' (not, we may note, 'carried out'; the terminology conveys the official anathema).

These may not be 'the innocent' necessarily: the attempt to transfer the notion of 'innocent civilians' from the international law of war to the study of terrorism has foundered on the realization that innocence is another relative, unstable quality. It was, for instance, impossible for people fighting against Germany in the Second World War to accept that most German civilians (with the exception of the regime's political opponents who were in concentration camps) bore no responsibility at all for the existence and conduct of the Nazi regime. They were assumed to be legitimate targets for indiscriminate blockade (as had been the less democratically empowered citizens of the much less criminal Second Reich during the Great War). Did they deserve even the protection from direct attack that international law guaranteed them, much less protection against indirect ('collateral') injury? (Not if you took the Churchillian line that 'they have sown the wind, they shall reap the whirlwind'.)

But of course the Germans themselves felt, if not entirely, then substantially (and increasingly) innocent: this amplified their sense of unfairness when they were deliberately targeted by the British bombers. And in politics, as distinct from courts of law, subjective belief and feeling are supreme. The feeling of innocence, together with vulnerability, form crucial elements in what may be called the 'process of terror' – the process by which violence generates political effects. This provides a key to what I shall call 'pure' terrorism. Targets may not be in an objective sense innocent, but they must be in practical terms defenceless ('soft'). The essence of terrorism is the use of violence by the armed against the unarmed. But how does this work?

The terror process

We can distinguish three elements in the process of terror:

(1) Seizing attention: shock, horror, fear, or revulsion

This is certainly the most straightforward stage. People's need for order and security impels societies to establish conventions and boundaries to regulate violent coercion: when these are transgressed, shock is generated. Moreover the special quality of terrorist acts – attacking the defenceless – dramatically magnifies the anxiety about security which is never far from the surface of society. Some writers have argued that fear as such is not a crucial factor – the mere excitement or fascination of violence may generate sufficient impact – and this may be true. But certainly without some sense of disturbance, of abnormality if not enormity, attention would not be seized.

(2) Getting the message; what do terrorists want?

This is a much more complex and less predictable element of the process. By no means do all terrorist groups rush to claim responsibility for their actions, or if they do so, deliver a comprehensible rationale or demand. When (presumed) 'terrorist' acts are left 'unsigned' – like PanAm 103 or the 9/11 attacks – it is up to the onlookers to fill in the blanks. The results can be varied. Controversy over responsibility for the destruction of PanAm 103 over Lockerbie, Scotland, in December 1988 has persisted ever since; in 2005, a senior Scottish police officer alleged that the evidence on which the Libyan Abdelbaset al-Megrahi was convicted in 2001 was planted. (The Scottish government's release of al-Megrahi on medical grounds in 2009 provoked an international incident.) George W. Bush assured his citizens that the September 2001 attacks were 'intended to frighten our nation into chaos and retreat'. But retreat from what, or where? American commentators, both official and unofficial, showed a marked reluctance to accept the fairly well-established view that Osama bin Laden's primary *casus belli* against the USA was the defilement of Saudi Arabia by the presence of US troops. Instead they preferred more abstract explanations of the attacks rooted in envy or hostility towards American prosperity and democracy. A special counsellor to the President, Karen Hughes, explained 'they hate us because we elect our leaders'. Even though Osama bin Laden had declared war on the USA in 1996, his specific charges (such as defilement of Muslim territory by US troops) were hardly considered. Indeed, his declaration was largely ignored for a decade, partly because it was, as Mary Habeck suggests, couched in language 'largely incomprehensible to non-Muslims'. The Spanish government tried to pin responsibility for the Madrid train bombing in March 2004 on ETA; (unusually) it suffered electoral defeat for its perceived deception.

There is clearly a difference between the comprehensibility of terrorist acts designed to achieve limited objectives, for example the release of an organization's members, or some specific political concession, and those whose objectives are revolutionary – whether in the social, spiritual, or ethnic sphere (rebirth, independence, and suchlike). These varied messages may be communicated by the violent act itself ('propaganda by deed'), but there is a strong likelihood of misunderstanding unless it is reinforced by a clear statement.

(3) Fight or flight? – the response

Partly because the assessment of motives can be quirky, responses can be unpredictable or contradictory. If the demands are comprehensible and fulfillable, fear may drive people to comply. Ordinary people may be able to fulfil minimal demands – to keep quiet and refuse to help the police, for instance – but bigger political demands can't usually be delivered by them. The people who are most likely to be intimidated or alarmed are the people who in most political structures are outside the decision-making sphere. (Those inside it, police or military chiefs and government ministers, are well protected and professionally debarred from panic.) Can public fear really change policy? Terrorists themselves often seem vague about this crucial link in the process.

Terrorism theorists have distinguished between 'targets' and 'resonant mass', the latter being presumed to be the force that could generate the sort of political pressure that might oblige governments to comply. (So fear, or fascination, must be focused tightly enough to ensure a connection; if its effect is too diffuse the mass will not resonate at the right frequency.) The degree and focal intensity of pressure required will vary according to the 'extremity' of the demand. Where there might be supposed to be a simple cost/benefit calculation – as for instance with the Irish Republican Army's (IRA) cherished notion that under consistent attack the British public would eventually decide that it was not worth maintaining British forces in Ireland – the process might in theory be straightforward. In practice, however, public reactions can be perverse. The reaction to the 1974 Birmingham pub bombings by the IRA, for instance, was not a demand for British withdrawal but an insistence on refusal to concede to violence. So there is an alternative third stage scenario in which, instead of securing compliance, terrorism provokes a violent state reaction – which will either destroy the terrorist organization or, by 'unmasking' the inherent violence of the system, destroy the state's own legitimacy.

Strategies of terror

Thinking about the terror process suggests that there are significant functional differences between what some writers have called 'types' of terror. In the 1960s, the pioneering work of T. P. Thornton proposed two basic varieties, 'enforcement' and 'agitational' terror. The function of enforcement terror is likely to be limited, aimed at preserving the security of the rebel organization by deterring the public from giving information to the security forces. To succeed in this, the organization needs a sufficiently extensive surveillance system to persuade people that assisting the authorities will be detected: most terrorist groups are simply too small for this. (On the other hand, the security of small clandestine groups is much easier to maintain by secrecy alone: only when an organization tries to interface with the public do its risks multiply significantly.) Thus enforcement terror has usually been a by-product of a guerrilla campaign – as it was in Ireland 1920–1, Vietnam 1945–50, Algeria in the 1950s, Palestine 1936–9 – where it was fairly easy for people to grasp terrorist requirements and at least partly comply with them.

> The great thing about anarchist vengeance is that it proclaims
> loud and clear for everyone to hear: that this man or that man
> must die for this and this reason; and that at the first opportunity
> which presents itself for the realization of such a threat, the rascal
> in question is really and truly dispatched to the other world.
>
> And this is indeed what happened with Alexander Romanov, with
> Messenzoff, with Sudeikin, with Bloch and Hlubeck, with Rumpff
> and others. Once such an action has been carried out, the
> important thing is that the world learns of it *from the
> revolutionaries*, so that everyone knows what the position is.
>
> Johannes Most, *Freiheit*, 25 July 1885

Agitational terror is likely to grasp at much more extensive,
longer-term goals: 'revolution' of some kind, or 'national
liberation'. Some of these goals are more feasible than others. In
the colonial context, a cost/benefit analysis may plausibly favour
a terrorist strategy, since imperial rulers may be prepared to cut
their losses and quit. In domestic politics, the stakes are usually
much higher – the survival of the political elite and its associated
hegemonic structure ('private property', 'capitalist institutions').
For this elite, no benefit is likely to weigh against the costs of
concession – so the struggle will probably escalate. Whereas
'compliance' may be secured by low levels of carefully targeted
violence, agitational violence will intensify, and targeting may
become indiscriminate in order to maximize shock. Here the
outcome depends on whether the terrorists are generally perceived
as public enemies or outlaws, *hostes humani generis*, with whom
no meaningful interaction is acceptable.

Thornton's basic typology remains persuasive, though later writers
have added further refinements. In an exceptionally lucid case
study of revolutionary terrorism focused on the Algerian FLN
(*Front de Libération nationale*; National Liberation Front),

Martha Crenshaw suggested that the support-building function of terrorism encompassed two quite distinct aims: first, securing obedience or compliance (what Thornton called 'enforcement'); and second, bidding for sympathy and ideological or moral endorsement. This 'inspiring' quality is often neglected, especially by conservative writers who are concerned to deny any legitimacy to terrorist action in pursuit of agitational or revolutionary goals.

Endorsement may be the objective not only of revolutionary but also of counter-revolutionary, right-wing, or reactionary terror, dedicated to the prevention of change or the recovery of a former political order. This 'white terror' is often precipitated by revolutionary change or the threat of it, and is characteristically pro-state – like, for example, the array of Ulster loyalist paramilitary groups – but if the state is seen as already under alien domination, such groups can be impelled to attack the state they claim to be defending. The most spectacular and disturbing outbreak of this syndrome in recent years is the libertarian or white-supremacist 'militias' in the USA, who hold that the federal government and its agencies, such as the FBI, are under the control of a 'Zionist world government' (or indeed lizards, for the surprisingly numerous adherents of David Icke) dedicated to the destruction of American liberty. Timothy McVeigh's retaliation against the FBI in Oklahoma City in 1995, the deadliest American terrorist act, must surely have been conceived as a rallying-call to bring Americans to their senses, to make them see how things really are. This stands, as we shall see, in a long tradition of propaganda by deed.

Terrorist action may be auxiliary – one element of a larger military or guerrilla strategy; it may be confined to limited goals (revenge, publicity, political statement, release of prisoners, ethnic autonomy); or it may be 'absolute' – the pursuit of political goals through the systematic use of terror alone. It is this absolute, independent terror strategy, rather than terrorist action *per se*, that should properly be labelled 'terrorism'. It has a unique logic, which we can trace across the last century. It was first distinctly outlined in Johannes Most's *Philosophy of the Bomb,* an anarchist tract of the 1880s, and rests on a number of connected propositions:

1) outrageous violence will seize the public imagination;
2) its audience can thus be awakened to political issues;
3) violence is inherently empowering, and 'a cleansing force' (as the later anticolonial writer Frantz Fanon put it);
4) systematic violence can threaten the state and impel it into delegitimizing reactions;
5) violence can destabilize the social order and threaten social breakdown (the 'spiral of terror' and counterterror);
6) ultimately the people will reject the government and turn to the 'terrorists'.

Thus terrorism properly so called is not just the use of violence for political ends; not just outrageous violence; not just violence by the armed against the unarmed; it is conceived as a free-standing, sufficient, and decisive political strategy.

Terror and politics

Thinking about the terror process leads to the conclusion that the essential distinction between war and terrorism lies in their operational logic: war is ultimately coercive, terrorism is persuasive. War is in essence physical, terrorism is mental. (This is not to say that war is exclusively a matter of physical force; even Clausewitz, writing at a time of highly formalized warfare, remarked that in war the moral is to the physical as four is to one. But if we were to hazard an equivalent ratio for terrorism, it might be more like four thousand, or indeed four million.) The point is that the physical power of terrorism can in principle be minuscule. Even in a major target of terrorist attack such as Israel, it has been pointed out, the fatalities and injuries to Israeli citizens from terrorist attacks since the 1967 war would barely deserve a separate

2. The Federal Building in Oklahoma City was a target that symbolized the power of government to its opponents in the Christian militias. It was bombed in April 1995, on the anniversary of the burning of the branch Davidian compound in Waco, Texas, during an assault by federal agents; but none of the 168 who died were members of the Bureau of Alcohol, Tobacco and Firearms which the building housed

line in the national mortality and morbidity statistics if their significance were purely quantitative.

Terrorism operates, therefore, through subjective psychological pressure. Its biggest facilitator is collective alarmism, a regrettably banal phenomenon that has been registered in the White House as well as middle-class suburbs and peasant villages across the world. The essential precursor of the Great Terror of the French Revolution was the 'Great Fear' which spread across France in the summer of 1789. This irrational panic was not only symptomatic of pre-modern society – as many 20th-century 'spy scares' demonstrated. Rumour remains one of the most subversive social processes.

Pure terrorism resolves the discrepancy between actual destructive power and desired political effect by an almost mystical belief in the transformative potential of violence. Some writers have identified this as the 'sacralization of violence'; but without requiring mysticism we can see that terrorist logic clearly rests on a symbolic conception of sociopolitical power relations. Here the complexities, delays, and mistakes of the regular political process can be shortcircuited, or we might say 'hotwired', by violence – which will lay bare the deeper reality of collective allegiance.

This simplified view of politics may also explain a problem set up by many writers on terrorism – how can terrorists (who far from being 'criminals, crusaders, and crazies' emerge in most good empirical studies as 'disturbingly normal' people) go out and kill innocent people in cold blood? A typical example is the assertion that terrorists need to be 'without the human emotions of pity or remorse'. This suggestion of moral deformity results from a false antinomy between 'cold blood' and the 'heat of battle' – the latter being what supposedly makes it possible for ordinary people to kill in war. Both these concepts are very treacherous. In the modern world, certainly, the ethical mechanism by which ordinary people have been able to set aside pity and remorse in order to kill other ordinary people has been symbolic generalization – the smothering of the victims' individual human qualities by their collective identity (whether religion, class, race, or ethnicity). Far from being at all monstrous (in the sense of unusual), this kind of stereotyping powered most, if not all, of the wars, genocide, and violent revolutionary struggles of the 20th century and remains the common currency of nationalist discourse and the motor of ethnic cleansing. If terrorists are 'fanatics of simplicity', so are all too many good citizens. Most terrorists, like all too many of those who have taken part in mass murder, are disturbingly normal.

Women and terrorism

Another striking contrast between terrorism and war has been the remarkable prominence of women in terrorist operations. From Vera Zasulich, who carried out the first *Narodnik* armed attack when she shot the governor of St Petersburg in 1878, to Waffa al-Edress, the first female Arab 'suicide bomber' in Israel in January 2002, women have been front-line actors and, consequently, pioneer recasters of gender roles. Indeed, something like a quarter of the Russian terrorists of the 19th century were women; a proportion possibly exceeded among the German and American terrorists of the 1970s. A full third (33%) of the Communists Organized for the Liberation of the Proletariat (COLP) in Italy were women, and 31% of that nation's *Brigate Rosse* (Red Brigades). Is this because terrorist actions, small-scale and not calling for traditional military 'combat', are inherently less physically demanding? Or because terrorist groups (with some notable exceptions) have tended to be progressive? Or merely because they are too small to generate the characteristic militarism or *machismo* of regular armies? It's hard to say: the few serious studies so far have focused on women's motivation rather than the dynamics of these organizations.

3. Waffa al-Edress, the first female Palestinian 'suicide bomber',
or self-martyr, wearing the insignia of al-Fatah before her mission to
a Jerusalem shopping centre

The prominence of women has been noticed from time to time (though we should note that even where they are prominent, they remain a minority), and seems to invite some explanation. One eminent authority on terrorism, Walter Laqueur, has recently offered the somewhat Olympian assertion that 'women terrorists are more fanatical and have a greater capacity for suffering. Their motivation is predominantly emotional and can not be shaken through intellectual argument.' Such speculations, which seem to hover close to traditional stereotypes, invite a number of questions; what, for instance, do we understand by the label 'fanatical'? The role of many women in 'martyrdom operations' (over one-third of Chechan suicide bombers between 2000 and 2010 were women, known as the 'Black Widows') may well be explained less extravagantly – revenge for the torture and killing of their brothers and husbands.

Geula Cohen, a fighter with the Zionist 'Stern Gang' (Lehi) in Palestine in the 1940s, offered this account of her first reading of Lehi's bulletin *Hechazit*:

> It was the first time in my life that the twenty-two letters of the Hebrew alphabet had arranged themselves on a page especially for me. I felt that I was writing rather than reading the words.

This was instant identification. Still she saw differences between herself and her male comrades.

> Whenever I accompanied any of the men as they set out for an action, I always noticed the same expectant gleam in their eyes and the same tense, yearning look on their faces, an anticipation of some longed-for object of sacrifice, and I knew that here was a spark of that primeval fire in which truth is born, . . . the kind of tension from which the artist surely springs.

For her, biology ruled that women were never born to be artists, or combatants: men would perform better on the battlefield not only because they were stronger,

> but also because their spirit thirsts more than yours does to vanquish the death which you shall one day conquer within your own body.

Chapter 2
Crusaders and conspirators

'You don't understand, mother,' said Alice, calm and
confident. 'We are going to pull everything *down*. All of it.
This shitty rubbish we live in. It's all coming *down*. And
then you'll see.'

Doris Lessing, The Good Terrorist (1984)

The good terrorist

At some stage in discussions of terrorism, we meet up with the
enigmatic figure of the 'good terrorist' – the ironic title of Doris
Lessing's attempt to get inside the life of one of the *groupuscules*
which infested Europe in the 1970s and 1980s (to whom we will
return in Chapter 4). Good terrorists are those whose actions are
justified by the oppressiveness of the system they oppose. A certain
admiration, however reluctant, marks even conservative accounts
of the modern pioneers of terrorism, the 19th-century Russian
populists: a recognition that unlike terrorists of the right, they
'genuinely believed in a free and nonviolent society'. This was the
key to their conviction, which can be plausibly attributed to nearly
all terrorists, that any change would be for the better.

Modern terrorists are rarely seen in this light. Like many of the
most durable prejudices, the stereotype of the terrorist as a

psychopathic monster has survived a lot of academic efforts to modify or erase it. Most academic studies point to the view that terrorists are generally remarkable for their sheer ordinariness. The qualities popularly supposed to be needed to carry out terrorist acts – at best a lack of pity, at worst a malign will to evil – are either not needed, or if needed are regrettably common. There have been arguments that a significant number of terrorists experienced difficult childhoods – like Doris Lessing's Alice – but these cannot (yet at least) be systematized. Most of the considerable energy devoted to writing about 'the terrorist personality' has so far been wasted.

So who becomes a terrorist? The answer is likely to be that it depends on the circumstances. Terrorist organizations differ markedly in how they recruit their members. Some (particularly the revolutionary kind) will indeed require fanatics, ideologues, dreamers; others (notably the nationalist kind) may be so embedded in their communities that recruitment resembles a rite of passage. For Geula Cohen, the Lehi (in which she became a leading recruiter) was a band of poets:

> The soldier was weighed down by his weapons... he could never catch up with the poet who took to the air, sustained in his flight by visions of higher worlds. Eventually, of course, the soldier would reach the point where the poet last stood, and he would hear echoes of the poet's song. From these echoes he would spark a conflagration.

The perfect deed of the good terrorist is assassination. Classical tyrannicide was valorized because it could remove the oppressor instantly and with the maximum precision. In complex modern states the assassin might pick a symbolic or a functional target – the monarch or his chief of police, say. The Russian revolutionary organization *Narodnaya Volya* (People's Will) struck at both, most famously Tsar Alexander II; and so launched a fashion that seemed, in the last couple of decades of the 19th century, to threaten (in bourgeois eyes) the whole civilized world. The readiness of these assassins to risk their own lives – in many cases a certainty of capture and execution – compelled a mixture of fascination, admiration, and horror. (As, a century later, has the emergence of 'suicide bombers'.) While it is useful to be reminded that terrorism is adopted because 'it works', this is not the whole story. 'A terrorist', as Italian researchers have suggested,

> does not simply weigh risks against the likelihood of success, as is normally the case, but adds into the equation the abstract value of the cause for which he or she is fighting. This is the reason why traditional notions of deterrence are ineffective against such a subject.

The first attempt to establish an international convention against terrorism was a response to the assassination of King Alexander of Yugoslavia in 1934. It was beset by the sort of problems evident in one British official's view of its purpose: 'to discountenance the use for political purposes of methods which all civilized opinion must condemn'. But who were to be the judges (and executioners) of civilization? The belief that there was some baseline criterion against which 'terrorist' methods could be identified was optimistic. As the same official also noted,

> If all states were at all times decently governed, presumably anyone who attempted by force to overthrow an existing government should be a *hostis humani generis*; but when the government is itself a terrorist government, I think a person who endeavours to overthrow it by the only means available is not necessarily to be so regarded.

Freedom fighters?

That one man's terrorist is another woman's freedom fighter – or one woman's terrorism is another man's heroism – is surely a commonplace of our times. A truism – but is it true? Can it help us to understand the nature of terrorism? Many writers on terrorism dismiss it out of hand, but we can usefully look at the reasons why such relativism has been so noticeable, and at ways of testing whether terrorism can really be a strategy of liberation.

There are some obvious grounds for relativism. Terrorism as a distinctive political concept got its name (and much of its unattractive reputation) from the actions of the holders of state power, perhaps the first modern regime – the French Convention of Year II of the French Revolution (1793–4). Since then, governments have been on any quantitative measure the most prolific users of terroristic violence (see Chapter 3). Yet there is no hint of this in the dominant official discourse, whether of national or international law. In that discourse, terrorism is used by extremists – rebels – against the established order – the state.

It has never been too hard to detect the hypocrisy or double standards in operation here, not just for anarchists with their insistence that the violence of their protests was puny in comparison with the 'violence inherent in the system'. As the 20th century wore on, most onlookers could not fail to notice that states threatened by far less extreme nationalist movements routinely branded their resistance methods as terrorism and ruled their perpetrators out of the realm of politics as moral outlaws. Sometimes, though, states did come to political terms with these 'thugs' and 'murderers' who allegedly owed their power to violent intimidation of the law-abiding majority. First and perhaps foremost of these outlaws brought in from the cold was Michael Collins of the IRA in 1921; but plenty more have followed.

Some observers have moved quickly from noting the hypocrisy of the state's use of the terrorist label to insisting on the equal – or greater – culpability of the state in the use of terrorist violence. Radical critics like Noam Chomsky and Richard Falk have projected a symmetrical image of reckless violence committed by rebels and governments alike. But it was not necessary to go this far to conclude that the promiscuous use of the terrorist label had by the 1970s robbed it of any precision or analytical value. It was simple enough too for 'terrorists' to hurl the label back at their accusers; thus the Jewish 'underground' denounced 'the British terror' and pronounced the British administration, army, and police in Palestine to be 'terrorist organizations'; in 2002, the al-Aqsa brigades declared themselves 'honoured' to be labelled a terrorist organization by the world's greatest terrorist, the US government. The 'terrorism-heroism' truism may have represented not just a suspicion that facts were being misrepresented, but also an acceptance that the reality was too complex to fit these rigid categories.

Freedom fighters need some way of overthrowing tyranny, oppression, or imperialism. Is terrorism a viable means of doing this? Modern terrorism really took off with a technological revolution that seemed to make almost anything possible – the invention of dynamite. This high explosive seemed to offer the prospect of reversing the crushing historic imbalance of power between oppressors and oppressed. Anarchists led the way in testing its efficacy. In 1886, for instance, the throwing of a bomb at police during an anarchist-led workers' demonstration in Chicago – killing a policeman and triggering a riot in which several other people were killed – created a huge sensation. The public impact of the event was tremendous. But what did it portend? Nobody admitted – much less claimed – responsibility. Still, when the anarchist activist Albert Parsons was arraigned for conspiracy to murder, he denied involvement but stoutly maintained in court that dynamite 'made all men equal and therefore free'. This was a heady message. Frank Harris used a hypothesis about the Haymarket explosion as the basis for his remarkable novel *The Bomb*, which presented a notably heroic and charismatic bomb-maker, Louis Lingg, as its key character. Significantly, Harris played up the concentrated destructive power of the new explosives to have Lingg make bombs small enough to hide in his mouth.

4. The idea of international terrorism erupted with the Haymarket bomb in Chicago on 4 May 1886, thrown at police breaking up a street meeting of anarchists – many of them recent German immigrants

So far, though, the faith placed in the destructive power that technology has placed in the hands of small groups, or even individuals, has been disappointed. Maybe the quantum leap possible in the future, with weapons of mass destruction (WMD), will change this. I shall try to assess this issue later in this chapter. But up to now, neither bombs nor any other technological miracles have made men free. Although the 20th century produced plenty of successful 'wars of national liberation', often with a significant terrorist dimension, none succeeded by terrorism alone. And the most striking failures have been those of the purest adherents to terrorist methods – the urban guerrillas of the 1970s and 1980s, the

German Red Army, the Italian *Brigate Rosse*, and so on – the result of whose campaigns has typically been not the overthrow of states but the intensification of state and public security measures, a general degradation in the quality of freedom.

Can terrorism liberate? Or might the process of terror have 'corrupting consequences that reverberate for decades'? Certainly the apocalyptic dreams which have animated many terrorist groups have never materialized. In this sense, those, like the distinguished historian Walter Laqueur, who argue that terrorism has always failed are right. Shock and horror have their limits. As in war, perhaps, the experience of violent conflict can shift social tolerances. Shock wears off, or at least some effects of shock are modulated; the initial idea that such a situation is intolerable and that something must break (a very pervasive initial reaction in stable, orderly societies) is replaced by a realization that it won't necessarily do so. Ordinary people probably wake up to this long before the terrorists. In Britain during the 1970s, there was a striking instance of this with the half-accepted, half-repudiated – but wholly unprecedented in public rhetoric – notion of an 'acceptable level of violence' by the IRA.

This was probably not meant to signal a let-up in the state's jealous monopoly of violence, so much as to argue the impossibility of dealing with terrorists. If we ask how political violence is 'normally' resolved in liberal-democratic polities, it is by the standard mix of controlled repression and limited concession. Terrorists, however, are mostly unamenable to limited concessions: it is by setting absolute, non-negotiable demands, as much as by using violence, that they opt out of the political process. Until they and the state can speak at least a few halting phrases in the same political language, the only response will be containment and coexistence rather than interaction. If terrorism cannot be eliminated, it must perforce at some level be tolerated – and it can be.

So is there a difference between terrorists and freedom fighters? On the historical record, those who have adopted a purely terrorist strategy have not been successful liberators. Conversely, the liberators – Collins included – were not pure or absolute terrorists. The crucial distinctions between terrorism and war point to the limited efficacy of terrorism in pursuit of radical objectives. Its corrosive and possibly corrupting effect on social bonds could in any case modify the operation of freedom itself. While we should still pay attention to Frantz Fanon's assertion of the liberating value of violence for the oppressed – 'it frees the native from his inferiority complex, his despair and his inaction: it makes him fearless and restores his self-respect' – the problem is that terrorist violence does not fulfil Fanon's democratic promise – 'liberation has been the business of each and all'. At the bottom line, its achievements have been negative: as Régis Debray lamented of those emblematic 'good terrorists' of the 1970s, the Tupamaros (see Chapter 5), they became 'the gravediggers of liberal Uruguay'.

International terrorism

In the 1980s, a new spectre arose to haunt the Western world: 'international terrorism'. Its emergence was heralded in the bizarre career of 'Carlos', a terrorist odd-job man who was turned by enterprising and imaginative journalists in the mid-1970s into a global phenomenon. Its shape was drawn above all by one book, Claire Sterling's *The Terror Network*, published in 1981, which traced a vast, unified global organization not only inspired but directly controlled by the USSR. This awe-inspiring perception chimed with the political rhetoric of the Thatcher–Reagan period: the struggle against the 'evil empire'. In 1981, the Secretary of State, Alexander Haig, accused the Soviet Union of 'training, funding, and equipping international terrorists'. Though he stopped short of the full Sterling measure, the concept of international terrorism was firmly established. Despite its obvious improbabilities, not to say absurdities, the terror network idea was subjected to surprisingly little criticism until the end of the Cold War eviscerated it.

Sterling achieved her effects by none-too-subtle sleight of hand – by omitting to define terrorism, she was able to incorporate a wide range of groups and incidents in her canvas. Following practice established by the CIA (which did at least have a clear definition of international terrorist events), she inflated her statistics by counting all acts, of any kind, of any group labelled as terrorist. Her standard of proof was undemanding. Most seriously, perhaps, she glossed over the historical and political context of terrorist groups, and the often sharp doctrinal differences between them. On the Sterling interpretation, the inherent fairness of Western societies meant that the only possible explanation for terrorist action was outside interference: there could be no real domestic terrorists.

Of course, it was undeniable that terrorism took on a distinctly international cast in the 1970s. The establishment of airliner hijacking as the most newsworthy terrorist action automatically internationalized the issue, and its pioneers, the Palestine Liberation Organization, were an international organization by default, since they were exiled from the land they claimed: as the US State Department still puts it, 'Palestinians are considered stateless people'. And they did indeed train in the Soviet Union, which did indeed, via its satellite states, supply them with equipment. Perhaps the most dangerous terrorist weapon of this time was Semtex ('magic marble'), a powerful 'plastic' explosive, invented by Stanislav Brebera in the Czech town of Semtin in 1966. Easy to cut and mould, usable in a wide range of conditions, undetectable by sniffer dogs, and available in a choice of colours, Semtex was (almost literally) a gift to terrorists. What dynamite had been to the late 19th century, Semtex was to the late 20th (only, unlike Alfred Nobel, its inventor did not make a fortune from it). During the 1970s, some 690 tonnes of Semtex were exported from Czechoslovakia to Libya alone, enough to make over a million bombs of the strength used to destroy PanAm 103 over Lockerbie in 1988; enough, as Presdent Havel ruefully admitted later, 'to support terrorism throughout the world for 150 years'. From Libya, then regarded as the USSR's key Third-World surrogate, it was certainly distributed to many terrorist groups, including ETA and the IRA. Such aid was a tremendous help to these organizations, but there is no evidence that it was decisive in keeping them active, much less in creating them.

Some terrorist organizations were distinctly international in outlook, but so of course had been their predecessors a century earlier. The assassination of President Sadi Carnot of France by an Italian anarchist in 1894, for instance, was in a sense paralleled by the actions of the German RAF and B2J in the 1970s – aimed at international capitalism and US imperialism (see Chapter 4). Such incidents as the assassination of Archduke Franz Ferdinand by a Serb at Sarajevo in 1914, or of King Alexander in Marseilles in 1934, were likewise international, certainly in the legal sense of

5. The emblematic drama of 'international' terrorism in the 1970s: a BOAC VC10, one of three airliners hijacked by the PFLP in September 1970, and destroyed on a Jordanian airfield

acts 'which disrupt international relations, and which the international community considers contrary to desirable norms of behaviour'. But in these cases, the description 'international' hardly describes the character of the groups involved, which were intensely nationalist.

There is a distinction between calculatedly 'international' actions and actions that happen, incidentally as it were, to cross national boundaries. For the latter – much the most common – events, many writers have used the term 'transnational'. But even though there is now a considerable literature on this topic, more often than not there is a lot of slippage between these key terms, and others such as 'global', which suggests that most writers still conflate them into a single phenomenon. The most careful systematic studies of this issue have stressed the difficulty of anything more than episodic cooperation between disparate terrorist groups; one has concluded emphatically that 'No "terrorist international" exists'.

A similar miasma of imprecision hangs about the associated term 'state-sponsored terrorism', much beloved of the State Department and conservative analysts. The heyday of this menace was the 1980s, when, according to one expert,

> communist states, especially the Soviet Union and their surrogates, as well as a number of other militant totalitarian regimes like Iran, Libya and Syria, are actively exporting terrorists and terror techniques into other countries... their activity is a manifestation of transnational state-sponsored terrorism. They indoctrinate, fund, train, arm sub-state groups of diverse national origins to act as their tools, using psychological warfare and propaganda to create severe psycho-social or political conflict in contemporary life.

One would need to ask how such opportunist action could produce such dire effects, and more level-headed writers have indeed suggested that a stress on the role of state sponsorship can be seriously misleading. The full-blown state sponsorship syndrome

> The terrorist is noble, terrible, irresistibly fascinating, for he combines in himself the two sublimities of human grandeur: the martyr and the hero. From the day he swears in the depths of his heart to free the people and the country, he knows he is consecrated to death. He goes forth to meet it fearlessly, and can die without flinching, not like a Christian of old, but like a warrior accustomed to look death in the face.
>
> Proud as Satan rebelling against God, he opposed his own will to that of the man who alone, amid a nation of slaves, claimed the right of having a will . . . The terrorist is immortal. His limbs may fail him, but, as if by magic, they regain their vigour, and he stands erect, ready for battle after battle until he has laid low his enemy and liberated the country. And already he sees that enemy falter, become confused, cling desperately to the wildest means, which can only hasten his end.
>
> Sergei Stepniak-Kravchinski, *Underground Russia* (1883)

has been likened to the discredited theories put forward by the French army during the Algerian war, portraying the Arab struggle as externally manipulated and denying the authenticity of indigenous nationalist motivation. US insistence on the central role of state sponsorship has survived such cautionary advice, however; and several of the old 'rogue states' have been recently re-identified by George W. Bush as part of an 'axis of evil'.

Superterror?

Can things get any worse? It has become clear over the last decade that we need to look into the future, to assess the possibility of terrorists acquiring and using so-called 'weapons of mass destruction' (WMD) – chemical, biological, and nuclear weapons. Although they did not involve such weapons, the unprecedented scale of the 9/11 attacks seemed to bring this exponential expansion of destruction a big step closer. The alarm had been raised some time earlier: in 1998 the US Secretary of Defense declared that 'the question is no longer if this will happen, but when'. In 1997, the National Defense Panel had urged that the army should refocus its attention on coping with major domestic emergencies, using the Army Reserve and National Guard to train local authorities in chemical and biological weapon contamination and detection, to assist in casualty treatment, evacuation, and quarantining, and in the restoration of infrastructure and public services after a disaster. President Clinton's 1999 budget assigned hundreds of millions of dollars to such response programmes as constructing decontamination units, stockpiling vaccines and antibiotics, improving detection methods for chemical and biological agents, and special forces training. As one commentator pointed out, 'the bill for these preparations could add up to tens of billions of dollars in the coming decades'.

In technological terms, the risks are undeniably increasing. The proliferation of nuclear weapons in the latter part of the 20th century began to dilute the monopoly of the superpowers. The collapse of the Soviet Union raised some worrying questions about the security of weapons and materials (especially the reported disappearance of a number of the KGB's special suitcase-sized bombs; though this may turn out to be due to poor accounting rather than theft or sale). And even if the security of military weapons could be guaranteed, it is not just weapons but knowledge that has proliferated. Fissile materials are harder to restrict. It seems likely that really determined terrorist groups could get hold of weapons-grade plutonium (Pu-239), though enriched uranium-235 (HEU) would be harder to obtain, and it is the latter that might more easily be detonated. The formidable problems of weapon-building, and indeed of delivery (which may defeat the capacity of most terrorist groups), may be partly circumvented by making so-called 'dirty bombs', designed to maximize contamination rather than explosive power. Deadly chemical and biological agents are also becoming easier to acquire. Once again, half the difficulty of using such weapons lies in delivering them, but it would be hard to argue that these difficulties can never be overcome – whether by skill or sheer luck. So the technical possibility of 'superterrorism' by WMD must be faced.

The question that needs to be raised, however, is one of psychology as well as technology: whether terrorists are really eager to use such weapons? And does this prospect, as a US judge declared as far back as 1981, entail 'a clear and present danger to the very existence of civilization itself'? Or is this another example of what critics see as deliberate drumming-up of public support for an aggressive foreign policy? There are certainly grounds for caution. A recent sceptical assessment of the threat suggested three major reasons why it might be exaggerated: sloppy thinking, vested interests, and morbid fascination. Most people fail to distinguish among the different types of terrorism, so that the 'prophets of doom' who pile all forms of terrorism into a single global menace make it seem far bigger and more coherent than it is. The real issue is not one of capability but of motivation: what political group could possibly benefit from using mass-destruction weapons? 'Only a rare, extremist mindset completely devoid of political and moral considerations will consider launching such an attack.' Of course, many people, including powerful interests like defence contractors – such as Dycor, manufacturers of contaminant monitoring systems – and indeed the burgeoning official counterterrorist establishment, are quite ready to suggest that many if not most terrorists fit this bill. Thirty years of study has, however, made clear that terrorism usually involves predictable rather than wild behaviour, and the vast majority of terrorist organizations can in principle be identified by fairly low-level intelligence systems.

Alarmism seems to be a natural by-product of media coverage of terrorism, and for the mass media superterrorism is an irresistible topic. 'People love to be horrified.' But this banal fact does not tell us very much about whether the thrill of fear has any rational basis. Nuclear, chemical, and biological weapons have a special capacity to get under people's skins: a visceral dread of poisons may be the reason why these weapons, unlike high explosives, have been categorized as morally unacceptable. If we make an inventory of the expanding range of technologies open to extremist organizations, there is plainly a wide scope for exploiting these potent phobias. And even if we may expect that most terrorists will continue to avoid such weapons for a mixture of moral and pragmatic reasons, there are several reasons why some terrorists might not. Religious extremists could find exemplars in the behaviour of gods like Jehovah, who visited his enemies with massive destruction, or holy men like Phineas (the core myth for some of the white supremacist groups known as Christian Patriots), who 'purified' the community by murdering the chief of his tribe. Millenarianism likewise can be impelled to demonstrative rather than instrumental violence. (Quite a lot of counterterrorist energy was expended on studying such groups in the last years of the 20th century, though the feared spate of activity in Y2K never materialized.) In the secular sphere, emulation of Hitler might well validate the use of mass destruction by neo-Nazi groups.

The latest work of one of the pioneers of the modern study of terrorism, Walter Laqueur, offers an even wider phalanx of potential users of WMD. A quarter-century on from his first work on the subject, which was notable for its sceptical, anti-alarmist tone, Laqueur is distinctly more pessimistic about the dangers posed by terrorism – or perhaps not 'traditional' terrorism so much as its postmodern half-sibling, the use of mass-destruction methods by individuals or small groups without any recognizable political agenda. WMD have undeniably transformed their power; the half-mad 'professor' of Joseph Conrad's *Secret Agent* and his real-life successor the 'Unabomber', may now no longer be marginal figures. But the sheer quirkiness, if not outright nihilism, of such 'terrorists' seems to undermine the possibility of any coherent response.

So though we may suspect that judges or politicians who proclaim 'a clear and present danger to the very existence of civilization' are distorting the traditional safeguards against the abuse of executive power, it is not at all simple to assess what kinds of financial and social costs should reasonably be paid to provide some sense of security. The financial costs have certainly become staggering, not just through the visible budgets of post-9/11 organizations like the US Department of Homeland Security – whose budget rose above $56 billion in 2011 – but also the incalculable economic costs of air travel security. But social costs could be higher still. Six months after the 9/11 attacks, the American jurist Ronald Dworkin warned that the biggest damage resulting from the counterterrorist reaction had been to the long-cherished American legal defences of individual freedom. Though nobody would dare to suggest publicly that such damage was greater than the mass killing in the Twin Towers, it may have a more pernicious long-term effect on the quality of our life.

Chapter 3
The reign of terror

Virtue without Terror is powerless.

Maximilien Robespierre, Year II

Eugene V. Walter's pioneering work on terrorism, an historical-anthropological study of the 19th-century Zulu state under King Shaka, set out a fundamental division between the 'regime of terror' and the 'siege of terror'. Though he focused on the operation of power in 'primitive societies', Walter's intention seems in part to have been to challenge the liberal assumption that naked violence can never provide the basis for a stable political regime. This was an important point to register about the role of violence in politics. Interestingly, though, it was a group of liberals who initiated the first modern regime of terror. Indeed, the first dictionary definition of the word 'terrorism' – '*système, régime de la terreur*' – was offered by the Académie française in 1798 in the light, plainly, of recent French experience. To get a perspective on the uses of political intimidation we need to start from this point.

Terror and purification

In its 'Year II' (1793–4), the French republic, born with the deposition and execution of King Louis XVI in autumn 1792, was under threat from foreign invasion and internal rebellion. In July 1792, the National Assembly had declared *la patrie en danger* (the fatherland in danger), and in August 1793 it decreed a *levée en masse*, mobilizing the whole French nation to defend the country. Finally, in October, it declared terror 'the order of the day', to preserve the revolution against its enemies, kings and aristocrats (though most of its 10,000-odd victims were to be ordinary people, whose main offence might be to support their local clergyman in his refusal to accept the state's reorganization of the Catholic Church). The Committees of Public Safety and General Security, even more than the Convention from which they sprang, represented the progressive avant-garde of the French Revolution. They pioneered representative democracy and equality before the law. It was their adoption of terror that first imprinted the word 'terrorist' in the political lexicon, and transformed the Revolution in the eyes of many outsiders from a liberating to a destructive force. At the same time, their rationalism itself drove them to rework the justification of political violence. They had to find justifications for violent killing, especially lynching – the most problematic kind of violence because the most threatening to an ordered society. In the circumstances of public alarm and excitement, such killings could not be prevented, but could not be allowed to appear random or motiveless.

Their motivation provides a key to the distinctive nature of modern terrorism. At one level, the revolutionaries may seem to have acted as crusaders or millenarians, waging holy war against the infidel. Revolutionary language often sounded like this, but there was a crucial difference. The Reign of Terror was informed by the Enlightenment assumption that the social order can be changed by human agency. For a long time, those who were prepared to defend the terrorists did so on the grounds that their action was rational, because inevitable, in the circumstances. Certainly the Revolution as the Jacobin elite saw it was under threat in 1792–3, confronted with both external and internal enemies. But this argument is weakened by the fact that the Terror reached its height, with the truly terrifying law of 22 prairial Year II (1794) – depriving the accused of the right to counsel or to call witnesses, and empowering the revolutionary tribunal to execute suspects on the basis of moral conviction – at a time when both these threats were receding. (A pattern that would reappear in future bouts of state terror, as we shall see.)

More telling still is the way that the radical revolutionaries defined – or invented – their enemies in relation to their special vision of the revolution. The men who dominated the Committee of Public Safety, Robespierre and Saint-Just, like the editor of *L'ami du peuple* Jean-Paul Marat, invested the people with a republican virtue that was often too sublime for the real world. They framed issues in absolutes and opposites: Robespierre's rhetoric invoked 'all the virtues and all the miracles of the Republic' against 'the vices and the absurdities of the monarchy'. Counter-revolutionaries were labelled monsters, ferocious beasts, vultures, leeches, or – if allowed human status at all – brigands, and were found even more frequently amongst the lower orders than amongst the aristocracy. There might be a monarchist or a 'non-juring' priest (one who refused to accept the Civil Constitution of the Clergy) under every bed. Along with these negative or visceral identifications went the positive identification of revolutionary justice, in the form of lynching. Marat argued from the outset that such killing was an imprescriptible right of the sovereign people: the natural violence required to resist oppression and preserve liberty against tyranny.

Altogether this provided an ideological charter for the most extreme action, without compunction or remorse. One of the Convention's commissioners (*Représentants en mission*) sent out from Paris to bring the provinces under control announced 'I am purging the land of liberty of these monsters according to the principle of humanity.' When the counter-revolutionary rebellion at Lyon was crushed in November 1793 and the city – renamed Commune-Affranchie – placed under an openly terrorist commission, one of its declared objectives was the 'extirpation of

Guillotine, elevée en Place du Carousel le 13 aoust 1792. Servant à punir les conspirateurs et ennemis de la Patrie

A Paris, chez Villain, et Valonais Md. d'Estampes et fabriquants de papiers en couleur rue St Jaques à la Ville de Reims. No. 8.

6. The beginning of the Terror in revolutionary France: the first execution by guillotine, in the Place du Carousel, Paris, 13 August 1792

fanaticism', that is, religion. The future police chief Fouché exulted, 'Lyon no longer exists!'

Purge, extirpation: such language permitted massacres like the ferocious assault on the rebellion in the Vendée by the 'infernal columns' of the Republican army – labelled genocide (*le Génocide franco-français*) by a recent historian, or the mind-boggling *noyades*, mass drownings in the River Loire. But what was such terror intended to achieve? And what did it achieve? Extirpation is different from intimidation or persuasion. Were the dead simply to be eliminated, or to serve as an awful warning *pour encourager les autres*? Were the terrorists just too pressed for time to attempt to convert the counter-revolutionaries, or did they think them beyond saving by force of argument? In trying to unpick this issue, we can begin to establish a basic repertoire of the functions of terror.

Three key motives may be identified: vengeance, intimidation, and purification. The 'punitive will' identified by historians of the Revolution operated at every level from private through local to national: the more general the level, the more exemplary the function, as violence became symbolic rather than personal. The function of violence as moral agency – very clearly enunciated by Marat, for instance – was the Revolution's most distinctive translation of premodern into modern political logic.

White, black, red terror

Did all this constitute, in fact, a 'system or regime of terror', as the Académie's definition had it? How effective was it? It is hard to say how far ordinary people were 'terrorized', or whether the level of actual public compliance – as distinct perhaps from rhetorical protestations of revolutionary fervour – was materially altered by the Terror. (Certainly, obedience remained erratic.) And it is also hard to be sure whether the 'terrorists' were a small group imposing their will on the public, or, as seems more likely, in effect the agents of public insecurity and anger. But even if it was a kind of mass self-terrorization, like the *Grande Peur* (Great Fear) which had swept through rural France at the start of the Revolution, it retained a distinct and perilous political logic: the notion that violence could change political attitudes.

The French Revolution's ruthless and systematic use of violence created a model for the application of terrorizing force by the holders of state power over the next couple of centuries. A recent college textbook on terrorism identifies three functional levels of state terrorism: intimidation (to discourage dissent and opposition); coerced conversion (to alter lifestyle [*sic*]); genocide – deliberate extermination of an entire class, ethnic, or religious group. Although the prime exponents of terrorism 'from above' were overtly repressive autocracies and despotisms, or radical revolutionary regimes like the Bolsheviks during the Russian Civil War, in times of crisis constitutional states have also unleashed ferocious repressive action – as in France during the crushing of the Paris Commune in 1871 and the June days of 1848. The USA tolerated (to say no more) the persistent, systematic terrorization of the Southern black community by the Ku Klux Klan, as well as the less dramatic use of intimidatory violence by employers against labour organizations.

This *sub rosa* 'white terror', as it is often called, in defence of established social or political orders forms a constant undercurrent in modern history. (Some prefer to say 'black', though whiteness nicely reflects both symbolic political colours like those of the Bourbons and Romanovs, and the actual garb of white-supremacist terrorists such as the Ku Klux Klan.) The efficacy of direct action became a kind of subtext to the dominant modern liberal narrative of the evolution of consensual representative institutions. Its most resonant exposition was provided by Georges Sorel, whose writings express (however unsystematically) a fierce hostility to the decadence of turn-of-the-century bourgeois civilization. Sorel became and remains sensational because of his explicit embrace of violence as the antithesis of bourgeois security: in his seminal *Reflections on Violence*, he held that the middle class was cowardly and always backed away from violence, which had the power to revitalize the great nations 'at present stupefied by humanitarianism'. His support for revolutionary syndicalism and the weapon of the general strike may suggest that he was a revolutionary, but he is more plausibly understood as a 'conservative moralist' – whose ultimate aim was to impel the middle class to recover something of its former dynamism. Thus Sorel's work offered intellectual aid not only to left-wing opponents of parliamentary liberalism but also to fascists.

It has been cogently argued that Italian fascism was not terrorist, either doctrinally or actually, though it was of course expressly committed to violence in the seizure and maintenance of state power. Its leading ideologue, Sergio Panunzio, in fact developed a theory of violence which (in contrast to Marx, Engels, and Lenin) carefully distinguished between licit and illicit violence. Licit violence was the use of force for revolutionary ends, in a situation that could best be characterized as civil war. Violence was applied directly to enemies of fascism, and, to the extent that it was intimidatory rather than directly coercive, its victims could avoid it by changing their political position. Terrorism, on the other hand, Panunzio defined as indirect violence, attacking the innocent – noncombatants, women, children, the old, the unarmed, the helpless – with the intention of intimidating others. He maintained that such indiscriminate violence was illicit, because its victims could not adapt their behaviour to avert it; perhaps a surprising prohibition for a fascist, but one to which the fascist regime seems to have by and large adhered after coming to power. Even the notorious Special Tribunal for the Defense of the State, though it clearly violated the procedural rules of justice prevalent in liberal democracies, was qualitatively different from institutionalized terrorism: the system was repressive but not terroristic.

The argument here turns on what Hannah Arendt accepted as 'the surprisingly small number and the comparatively mild sentences meted out' by the Tribunal, which in the 17 years of its existence (from 1926 to 1943) passed no more than 47 death sentences, some of which were not carried out. But statistics are tricky here: what total might be regarded as the numerical threshold of terrorism? As with other forms of terror, crude numbers may be less significant than atmosphere. Many people still think that the Fascist *squadristi* created a 'reign of terror' sufficient to subvert the parliamentary system in the early 1920s. The exact reach of terror, and its relation to measurable violence, remains obscure. Clearly, the homicidal will and performance of both Nazi Germany and Stalin's USSR were vastly, almost immeasurably greater than Italy's. But was it just the scale of destruction that made them terrorist regimes? It may be that Italian Fascism's exaltation of violence, its ethos of war both external and internal, its remorseless attempt to project combat into all spheres of life, sufficiently undermined stable social expectations as to qualify as terrorist in effect if not in intent.

Hitlerism and Stalinism are both routinely categorized as terrorist regimes, but as with the French original, there is a question over how far their conduct represented terrorist manipulation rather than popular will. It certainly resulted in the mass murder not only of declared opponents but of groups unilaterally, often incomprehensibly, designated as public enemies (*Reichsfeinde* in Nazi parlance) or threats. Elimination and intimidation may be logically distinct, but in practice this programme served to paralyse oppposition and enhance the state's freedom of action. The same was true of the equally murderous regime of Stalin in the USSR. The arraignment of hundreds of thousands of people before Soviet Special Boards, whether as class enemies (Kulaks, for instance) or suspected spies or 'members of the family of a traitor', certainly lacked any of the safeguards of 'due process' – and often any specific charge – and served to crush all open political dissent. The breadth of the possible indictments created a climate of fear, and the process of indiscriminacy was taken to its limit in 1938 with the idea of targeting 'the silent' – those who had precisely avoided political commitment of any kind. Yet its purpose, at least as implied by chief prosecutor Vyshinsky himself, was elimination rather than intimidation: 'When it is a question of annihilating the enemy, we can do it just as well without a trial.'

The deadly pinnacle of genocide, the special crime of the 20th century, can be seen as the ultimate stage of terrorist regimes. Mass murder is unquestionably a terrifying phenomenon; but there may be problems in classifying genocide – as distinct from mass murder – as a terrorist act. Its very modernity points to its logic, which is ethnic rather than ideological. The Turkish roundup of Armenians during the First World War has been regarded as genocide by those who do not accept the Turkish state's explanation that it was a national security measure triggered by the danger posed by manifest Armenian disloyalty. It seems fairly clear, though, that on any explanation the objective was not to intimidate the Armenians (or by example any other national minority within the Ottoman state), but primarily to remove the strategic threat they respresented. This was done cruelly and recklessly, and the government was certainly responsible for tens or hundreds of thousands of deaths, even if it did not directly order the harshness of local implementation.

In the same way, it does not make sense to read the Nazi measures against the Jews as terrorist, although this is routinely done, as in the assertion that 'Hitler terrorized the Jews into submission' – as if he faced a problem of Jewish resistance. In fact, Nazi laws, by specifically ruling out assimilation, eliminated the possibility that Jews could adapt their behaviour (even to the extent of abandoning their religion) to avoid persecution. Nazism required not political, religious, or ideological, but biological, uniformity – and this lay outside the realm of political adaptation. Although Jewish submission was useful to the German authorities, it was not their goal. Their aim was a 'purification' which echoed that of the first terrorist regime in revolutionary France, but indirectly: the purity pursued here was not of virtue but of blood.

Still, the myth of the Fascist and Nazi seizures of power (*Machtergreifung*) remains the strongest support for what is probably the most potent fantasy of terrorism in the modern age. In his clear-headed analysis, Thornton identified 'disorientation' as 'the objective *par excellence* of the terrorist', suggesting that it is achieved partly by successfully demonstrating that the incumbent regime cannot guarantee order, and still more by the destruction of the social framework. Hannah Arendt said that the ultimate point of the terrorization process is the isolation of the individual from customary social supports. If terrorism could achieve this, it might create a situation in which the atomized masses eventually turn to the terrorists themselves as saviours. Enforcement terrorism can operate through the machinery of the state (whether open or secret) or through the more or less spontaneous action of vigilantes – to which the state sometimes turns a blind eye.

It is important to grasp how far state terror has dwarfed the puny efforts of rebels in the 20th century. (Only the Vietminh and Vietcong rivalled incumbent regimes in statistical terms.) Most writing on terrorism, focusing on anti-state actions, tends to sidestep this point; for instance, 'state terrorism' occupies only 13 of the 768 pages in the *Encyclopedia of World Terrorism* (1997), and 5 of those are about 'state-sponsored terrorism', a rather different phenomenon. (But at least this section is there; in many studies of terrorism it is not.) State terror may not fit the common model of clandestine terrorism, but it may well have played a bigger role in undermining liberal norms and public confidence.

In combination, the Contra forces have systematically violated the applicable laws of war throughout the conflict. They have attacked civilians indiscriminately; they have tortured and mutilated prisoners; they have murdered those placed hors de combat by their wounds; they have taken hostages; and they have committed outrages against personal dignity.

Americas Watch, *Violations of the Laws of War by Both Sides in Nicaragua* (1985)

The atrocities I had heard about were not isolated instances, but reflected a consistent pattern of behaviour by our troops. There were unit commanders who openly bragged about murders, mutilations, etc.... They told me it was the only way to win the war; that the best way to win the loyalty of the civilian population was to intimidate it and make it fearful of us.

Edgar Chamorro, Affidavit submitted to the International Court of Justice, 1985 (*in re* Nicaragua v. United States of America)

Free-range terrorism

The military or military-controlled regimes in Chile, Argentina, Peru, Brazil, Uruguay, and elsewhere, taking the socialist threat as justification, unleashed full-blown systems of terror designed to paralyse all left-wing activity. The keynotes of these systems, in which whole armies and police forces seem to have participated enthusiastically, were not only killing, but a perhaps more sinister and subversive structure of arbitrary imprisonment, torture, and 'disappearance'. Though these must be described as 'systems' of terror, they were not comprehensible as such – rather the apparently uncontrolled action of variegated and overlapping security forces created a nightmarish situation that may perhaps be called Kafkaesque.

For Chileans, who had prided themselves on their democratic traditions, the whole 'system' was terrifyingly capricious. At its dark heart, though, was an eruption of brutality that was far from Kafka's imagination. An Amnesty investigation following the wave of mass arrests in 1973–4 reported that

> methods of torture employed have *included* [*sic*] electric shock, blows, beatings, burning with acid or cigarettes, prolonged standing, prolonged hooding and isolation in solitary confinement, extraction of nails, crushing of testicles, sexual assaults, immersion in water, hanging, simulated executions ... and compelled attendance at the torture of others.

Within a short time, an equally formidable system of terror (called 'total terrorism' by one observer) emerged in Argentina. Here, as in Guatemala, El Salvador, and Nicaragua, terrorism – commonly known as 'the Process' – was used not only by the state but also by rebels and free-floating 'death squads' formed to bolster the state's repressive efforts. Whereas the rebel ERP (*Ejército Revolucionario del Pueblo*; People's Revolutionary Army) and Montoneros killed some 700 people (according to government figures), more than half of them military personnel, the 'Triple A' death squad, established under the Perón regime, probably killed over 2,000. The AAA achieved a dramatic intensification of a tradition of sporadic quasi-fascist terrorist action by *grupos de choque* against socialists and strikers over half a century before the 1970s. (The Peronist labour syndicates also maintained their own paramilitary groups.) After the military takeover in 1976, the AAA was absorbed into an infrastructure of state terror whose victims came from almost all sectors of Argentine society. By mid-1976, abductions were running at an average of over five a day, and at least 9,000 *desaparecidos* never reappeared. In all, the military regime killed somewhere between 10,000 and 30,000 of its people.

This regime involved a definite shift from the traditional terrorism of the shock groups – primarily assassination – to a large-scale campaign to root out 'subversion'. Its breadth stemmed from the characteristically broad notion of subversion held by military officers: General Videla defined as a terrorist 'not just someone with a gun or a bomb, but also someone who spreads ideas that are contrary to Western and Christian civilization'. The military regime set up some 340 secret detention camps where suspects were tortured and eventually disposed of – many of them thrown into the sea from aircraft – after giving information leading to further abductions. The secrecy may not itself have been deliberately designed to spread fear so much as to avoid the international condemnation that had afflicted the Chilean junta, but along with the institutionalization of torture it inevitably had that effect. Robert Cox, a perceptive journalist who witnessed the effects of the disappearances, wrote that 'it is difficult for the mind to grasp their awesome significance'.

What needs to be noted about this military 'crusade' is that it really got going after the threat to which it was a response had receded. Cox thought that the main explanation for the whole process was incompetence: 'The security forces were so inept in dealing with terrorism that they were driven by desperation to extreme methods and found themselves mimicking the terrorists.' But there was also the ever-present dynamic of vengeance. The guerrillas may 'only' have killed six or seven hundred people, but these included three federal police chiefs, five army generals, two admirals, and five senior air force officers. One of the most feared of the army commanders, whose sister was killed by rebels, became known as 'El Vengador'.

Ultraterrorism

Latin American death squads operate as an auxiliary to the counterterrorist actions of the state; but a potentially more irreconcilable matrix of terrorism has appeared in situations where a significant group, formerly dominant, sees itself as threatened with abandonment by the state itself. This sense of betrayal has emerged where settler communities face the prospect of a negotiated settlement between the government and rebel terrorists, as happened in acute form in French Algeria towards the end of the FLN's independence campaign, and in a more diffuse way in Northern Ireland during the protracted and inconclusive 'peace processes'.

Algeria presented an acute problem because the overall prospects for eventual integration of the French community – the *pieds noirs* – within an independent FLN-controlled state were not bright. The stakes were high, and the settler community, like the army, was convinced that the military struggle against the FLN had already been won. When the hope that the return of Charles de Gaulle to politics would cement this victory in political terms proved false, a group of senior army officers, together with some *pied noir* leaders, formed the OAS (*Organisation d'Armée Secrète*; Secret Army Organization) in 1960 with the aim of provoking a rebellion amongst the Algerian French, or at least halting the government's negotiations with the FLN. These people were undoubtedly impressed by the way FLN terrorism had worked, though they do not seem to have formulated any clear strategic theory of how it might achieve their own very different objectives. They were able to build up a murderous campaign in Algeria itself, whose most distinctive weapon was the new plastic explosives. By November 1961, the OAS could mount some 300 *plasticages* a month; and it killed 230 Muslims in a single week in May 1962. But the process of negotiation proved less vulnerable than many expected (Muslim retaliation was carefully controlled by the FLN), and the closest the OAS came to its aim of generating a settler revolt was a series of bloody but ineffective clashes between civilians and French troops in the Bab el Ouad quarter of Algiers.

The next step was to carry its attacks into metropolitan France, though the likely political effects of this were even more obscure. De Gaulle himself was an obvious target, but in fact, despite its carefully cultivated image of paratroop-style effectiveness, most of the campaign turned out to consist of uncoordinated and often pointless *plasticages* that made the OAS not only unpopular but ridiculous. Poor public-relations work left the impression that most of its actions were mere revenge, *règlements de compte*. The overall effect of OAS terrorism was, perhaps inevitably, counterproductive: it strengthened de Gaulle's position and allowed him to institute direct election for the French presidency (a key point in his reconstitution of the Fifth Republic); and it eliminated any viable future for the French population of Algeria (as well as making their reception in France distinctly chilly). But in the end, perhaps, none of this was the point. In the French army, whose refusal to back the rebels was crucial in preserving the Republic, some officers came to profess regret at their lack of courage. The rebel leaders were later incorporated in a nostalgic colonial cult: they had kept faith with the native Algerians (200,000 of them, in fact) whom France had recruited into the colonial army, and then abandoned; they became exemplars of moral integrity rather than careerism and legality.

The OAS did not provide a particularly inspiring model for reactionary activists, but it seems that such models play a less formative role on the right than on the left. What may be called 'vigilante' terror can emerge without any developed ideological basis. An important and problematic example is the Loyalist terror campaign which began in Northern Ireland around 1966, in reaction to nationalist celebration of the fiftieth anniversary of the 1916 rebellion and the improving north-south relations signalled by the meetings between Sean Lemass and Terence O'Neill. The driving impulse for such organizations as the Ulster Volunteer Force – which borrowed the name of a famous citizen militia in the pre-1914 crisis over Irish Home Rule, but which unlike the IRA had no direct organizational continuity – was to preserve the status quo and block any change in Northern Ireland's constitutional status. Although some efforts were made to provide later Loyalist paramilitary groups (notably the Ulster Defence Association) with a more sophisticated political programme, based on a British civic ideology, their fundamental motivation remained negative – against Irish nationalism. The profile of Loyalist violence was distinctly sectarian, in that the Catholic community was identified as the support base for the republican campaign. Unlike the OAS, Loyalist groups did not attempt to attack the government or British targets – though they were clearly suspicious of Britain's commitment to preserving 'the Union'. Most Loyalist operations were local; the spectacular car-bombing in Dublin in 1974 was an exception, yet this was arguably a very effective operation in its impact on 'southern' Irish opinion. The long-running and murky story of 'collusion' between some British security forces and the Loyalists is still unfolding, but suggests that the paramilitaries had some reason to believe that the state was on their side.

Running through any account of state terror is the tension between 'terror' as a semi-random by-product of massive repressive violence, and terror*ism* as a deliberately focused product of demonstrative violence. One notable authority suggests that 'rule

7. The explosion in South Leinster Street, Dublin, was one of three car bombs placed by Ulster Loyalist paramilitaries on 17 May 1974, killing 33 people altogether: a deadlier operation than any by the Irish Republican Army

by violence and intimidation by those already in power against their own citizenry' is 'generally termed "terror" in order to distinguish that phenomenon from "terrorism", which is understood to be violence committed by non-state entities'. Oddly, it seems that the former – vastly more murderous and widespread over the last century – has raised less public alarm than the latter. There was perhaps some consistency in the Soviet view in the early 1980s (inevitably dismissed as ludicrous special pleading by most Western writers at that time) that while communists embraced revolutionary violence, they 'reject terrorism as a means of obtaining political objectives'; and that the main perpetrators of terrorism in Afghanistan were the US-backed guerrilla forces.

Chapter 4
Revolutionary terrorism

Il n'y a pas d'innocents.

Émile Henry, 1894

Eugene V. Walter's second category of political violence, the 'siege of terror', represents the way in which terrorism is most commonly conceived: as a strategy of assault on the state. From this perspective we can see emerging in the 19th century an increasingly well-defined strategy in which terror forms the central – indeed, in the purest form, the exclusive – method. The word 'revolutionary' has been applied over the last century in three distinct kinds of social-political contexts: within existing nation-states; in external colonial situations; and in 'internal colonial' situations where one or more ethnic groups are oppressed by a majority group within a single (or not easily divisible) 'homeland'. But the criteria for truly revolutionary change – social transformation, or at least major social and economic change – are generally fulfilled only in the first of these circumstances. In cases where ethnic identity rather than progressive ideology is the driving force, resistance movements can be remarkably conservative – if not indeed reactionary. In this chapter and the next, these contrasting motives and goals will be explored.

Once again, the definition of revolution itself is not straightforward. Some writers prefer to set out a spectrum of revolutionary aims and outcomes, ranging from total social transformation to change of the ruling general or dictator – the so-called 'palace revolution'. Now and again there are revolutions from the top – *coups d'état* – but the common sense of the concept relates to political action from outside the incumbent power structure. A sensible general definition might be 'the attempt to seize political power from the established regime of a state, to bring about fundamental political and social change'.

Two ages of terrorism: 1

Terrorism with this aim emerged as a consistent and coherent strategy in the late 19th century. We need to recognize that this kind of terrorism was qualitatively new, a phenomenon essentially distinct from political assassination as practised continuously throughout history; not so much because of new technology or methods, but because modern terrorists had a different view of their role, of society, and of the significance of their actions. The concept of 'individual terror' is a key indicator of the modern age of violence. The label was pejorative, admittedly; it was attached to this form of terror in the early 20th century, a while after its heyday, by the Bolsheviks – who disapproved not of the violence as such but the individualism, the 'voluntarism' of the Socialist Revolutionary (SR) terrorist strategy in Tsarist Russia. Marx and Engels themselves had been oddly vague in their use of the concept of terror; they often conflated it with force or violence in general, which seems to be what Marx had in mind when he said that 'revolutionary terrorism' was the only way to shorten the 'agonies of the old society and the birth pangs of the new'. Lenin was far more careful, and produced an interesting definition of terrorism as 'single combat' in contrast to mass action. He branded terrorist campaigns as nonsensical, because such individual acts of violence were 'unconnected with the mass of the people'.

This view, albeit hostile, highlights the essence of the phenomenon that evolved through the parallel activities of anarchists, populists, and syndicalists, as well as nihilists in Lenin's youth. Though few of them acted absolutely alone, they were certainly very small groups with very big ideas about the recasting of society. They believed that individuals could change the course of history. They did not major on the term 'terror', though the leading theoretician of armed action in the *Narodnaya Volya* (People's Will), Nikolai Morozov, accepted the phrase 'terroristic warfare' on the grounds that this was an expression adopted by the people. The SR party programme in 1879 talked of 'destructive and terroristic activity'. But many alternative terms were used, some more or less euphemistic: Morozov advocated the term 'neo-partisan warfare' (with its echoes of the great patriotic struggle of 1812 against Napoleon), while the anarchists adopted the striking formula of 'propaganda by deed', Pilsudski's Polish Socialists called it the 'armed deed', and syndicalists 'direct action', or *reprise individuelle*.

The notion of propaganda by deed, first described by the Italian Federation of the Anarchist International in 1876, is a good place to start, because it vividly displays the underlying logic of so much terrorist action. The 'insurrectionary deed', 'designed to promote the principles of socialism by action', was (the Italian anarchists suggested) 'the most efficient means of propaganda and the one most capable of breaking through to the deepest social strata'. The idea of economy of means – very appealing to organizations too cash-strapped to exploit the conventional media of communication – is prominent here. In any case, the level of general literacy in 19th-century Europe imposed sharp limitations on conventional propaganda, as the French anarchist Paul Brousse lucidly argued the following year (1877) when he said that propaganda by deed could show 'the weary and inert masses . . . that which they were unable to read, teach them socialism in practice, make it visible, tangible, concrete'.

Though Errico Malatesta's original instrument of violent propaganda was insurrection rather than terrorism, repeated failures of insurrectionist attempts in Italy and elsewhere throughout the 19th century pointed unmistakably in the direction of the latter. And if we ask how death and destruction could 'teach' socialism, Prince Peter Kropotkin, the most rational and humane of the Russian anarchists (generally a rational and humane lot), thought he had a persuasive explanation. 'Actions which compel general attention' led the new idea to 'seep into people's minds'. A single act could 'in a few days, make more propaganda than thousands of pamphlets', and,

> Above all, it awakens the spirit of revolt; it breeds daring...Soon it becomes apparent that the established order does not have the strength often supposed...The people observe that the monster is not so terrible as they thought...

This effect, Kropotkin believed, would be strengthened rather than negated as the regime reacted with 'savage repressions' – which would 'provoke new acts of revolt, individual and collective, driving the rebels to heroism'. At the same time, Kropotkin was fiercely critical of random individual terror, cautioning that 'a structure based on centuries of history cannot be destroyed with a few kilograms of explosives'.

Despite this reservation, the central threads of the logic of revolutionary terrorism can be seen in Kropotkin's analysis. First, the power of the violent act not only to attract attention but also to convey quite a complex political message; second, the potential receptivity of 'the people', the masses or the workers, to the message, the assumption that their revolutionary awareness will accelerate as soon as 'the scales drop from their eyes'; and finally, the inevitability of a spiral of provocation and reaction that will radicalize the masses and eventually mobilize them into action against the government. This logic was embraced by both anarchists and populists, and imposed a number of strict conditions on the behaviour of terrorists. To delegitimize the state, revolutionaries had to select targets that would be perceived as legitimate by the people. To impress and convert the people, the revolutionaries must display the highest moral qualities – the 'heroism' referred to by Kropotkin. (There may also have been a streak of elitism here; terrorist action would keep the revolution under the control of the educated minority.)

Terrorist activity, as announced by the *Narodniki* (Populists) in 1879, began with careful targeting. It had two modes: 'the destruction of the most harmful persons in the government, and the punishment of official lawlessness and violence', and also 'the protection of the Party from spies'. Its aim was 'to break down the prestige of government' and 'to raise the revolutionary spirit in the people, and finally to form a body suited and accustomed to warfare'. Acquiring military skills and familiarity with high explosives was important to the ultimate outcome of the revolutionary struggle, but it was subordinate to the moral qualities of individual revolutionaries in the thinking of the *Narodniki*. Peter Lavrov's essay on 'The Social Revolution and the Tasks of Morality' (1884) put this clearly: 'We need energetic, utterly dedicated people, prepared to gamble all, to sacrifice everything. We need martyrs . . .' Because those using violence had 'no right to endanger the moral stance of the socialist struggle', he insisted, 'not one unnecessary drop of blood shall be spilled'. The justification, indeed the necessity, of armed action seemed self-evident in Tsarist Russia. Alexander Ulyanov (Lenin's older brother), who was arrested and executed in 1887 for his part in the planned assassination of Tsar Alexander III by a fringe group, the terrorist faction of the *Narodnaya Volya*, explained to his distraught – and highly respectable – mother, 'What can I do, mother, if there is no other way?'

The next generation of terrorists, the Combat Organization of the Socialist Revolutionary Party, stuck to these ideals. (Though, sadly for the Party, the Organization was run by a government double agent.) Grigori Gershuni said that for the SRs, 'anyone who does not demonstrate opposition to the crimes of the regime becomes by virtue of this fact an accomplice in their crimes'. But he still did not make this a charter for indiscriminate terror. He insisted that attacks had to be seen as just acts of retribution by the people, expressions of their true aspirations; 'only a revolutionary party which does not breach the revolutionary morality contains the force of life'. Most importantly, he gave an especially rapt expression to the essential belief of terrorists in their power to transform the world: 'Only a scientist who discovers a new law of the universe experiences a similar feeling, since this enables him to turn from slave to master of the universe.' Thinking of a prisoner who resists the worst torture, he demanded 'has he not subdued all the universe to his spirit?' 'A socialist party can win only by moral integrity, not by physical predominance.'

The most celebrated exemplar of this strict moral stance was Ivan Kaliayev, the assassin of Grand Duke Sergei, who refused to throw his bomb when he saw that the prince's family was in the carriage with him (though he succeeded in killing him in a later, suicidal attempt). Assassination remained the lodestar for these revolutionaries, who preserved for a generation the belief that, as one of the assassins of Tsar Alexander II recorded, the Tsar's death would be 'the final awful blow ... It will deal a mighty blow to that system which some sly souls call "absolute monarchy" but which we ourselves call tyranny.'

Gradually, though, it became clear that the original logic of the 'blow at the centre' was flawed. Tsar followed assassinated tsar, and the supply of candidates to become chief of police showed no sign of drying up, however often they were attacked. Though anarchists ceaselessly picked over the vulnerabilities of the state's lines of communication, the sad truth seemed to be that the most repressive states were the least vulnerable to terrorist attack – precisely because there public opinion was politically insignificant. Democracies were far more sensitive, but high-minded terrorists excluded them from their list of targets. At the fifth SR conference in 1909, the party's principal theoretician,

Chernov, worried that 'we must not allow routine to set in. Terror is a form of military combat, a form of war.' In war, Chernov said, states whose military methods were outdated exposed themselves to defeat, so in internal warfare 'we must master modern techniques' if terror was to remain 'terror in the true sense of the word'. Here was the origin of a process of self-deception, continuing over the next century, in which revolutionary terrorists disguised the implications of failure by continually appealing to the possibilities of new and more destructive technology.

In the wave of anarchist terror that swept the Western world around the turn of the century, it was already clear that one compensatory mechanism was to abandon restraints on targeting choice. For anarchists, the distinction between despotic and liberal-democratic states was illusory: the enemy of human freedom was the state itself. Following the doctrine of 'anarchist vengeance' proclaimed by the exiled German anarchist Johannes Most in his paper *Freiheit* in London and then New York through the 1880s, anarchists slid away from Russian notions of tyranny and attacked the representatives of liberal states. In 1893, Auguste Vaillant threw a bomb into the French Chamber of Deputies, which he denounced as 'corrupt'. (Perhaps after the Panama Scandal French public opinion may have been inclined to agree. Although Vaillant failed to kill any of his targets, he became an anarchist martyr, who had 'never stolen or killed'.) But the promiscuous spread of killing seemed ever more nihilistic. The French Republic's president, Sadi Carnot, was assassinated by an Italian anarchist exile, Santo Caserio, in 1894; and in 1901, President McKinley of the USA was killed by a Pole. Indeed, anarchist terrorism was as active in the USA as anywhere: Most's exhortation to 'murder the murderers' found plenty of outlets in the struggle of workers to organize in the face of ruthless strikebreaking action by employers.

Still more indiscriminate targets were also chosen. In 1893, the Liceo Theatre in Barcelona was bombed and 20 of the audience killed. The defining rationale, 'there are no innocents' – at least among the bourgeoisie – was coined the following year by the French anarchist Émile Henry after hurling a bomb into a Paris café. The young shoemaker Léon-Jules Léauthier at the same time declared 'I shall not strike an innocent if I strike the first bourgeois I meet'; 'Would it make any difference which *bourgeois* one throws the bomb at?', a Russian anarchist asked rhetorically in 1907.

Two ages of terrorism: 2

After a generation in which terrorism seemed to be engulfing the world, it suddenly went out of style. (Annual totals of SR terrorist incidents in Russia, for instance, dropped from 51, 78, and 62 in 1905–7 to 3, 2, and 1 in 1908–10.) The culminating act of the first age of terrorism, the Sarajevo assassination (discussed in the next chapter), launched the war that pushed terrorism back to the sidelines of political action. For instance, James Connolly, the only socialist among Irish revolutionaries, who set up a fighting organization in 1913 (the Irish Citizen Army), seems never to have considered adopting a terrorist strategy. He wrote combative essays on 'street fighting' which paid lip-service to modern technology, but fundamentally harked back to the days of the popular 'barricade revolutions' of the 19th century. The haemorrhage of the First World War seems to have drained Western society's capacity for shock. The decline of anarchism, and the replacement of the SRs in Russia by the Bolshevik regime, redrew the paradigm of revolutionary action. This was most potently the case with the doctrine of 'protracted war' enunciated by Mao Zedong in China during the 1930s. There was no role – in theory at any rate – for terrorism in this idea of methodical mass mobilization.

A revival of terrorism looked unlikely. Aside from sporadic and often desultory campaigns like those of the IRA in the late 1930s and 1950s, terrorism as a freestanding strategy was absorbed into larger-scale revolutionary movements which, whatever their official theoretical labels, were essentially nationalist mobilizations. Most of the resistance movements during the Second World War were fighting national struggles; and few people, apart from the Germans, described resistance fighters as terrorists. (In a notable study of partisan methods written at the end of the war, the word 'terrorism' appeared only as a description of German antipartisan methods.) After the war, Marxist revolutionary movements proliferated, but their basis often remained national. The Malayan People's Liberation Army, for instance, whose members were curtly labelled 'Communist Terrorists' (CTs) by the British authorities, failed to extend its revolutionary appeal beyond the marginalized Chinese community in Malaya. Though its leadership was certainly communist, it could not construct the kind of cross-ethnic class solidarity which Marxist revolutionary theory required. Here, as elsewhere in the postwar world, the threat of 'communism' which so terrified the First World, if it existed at all, lay almost entirely in the dynamism and discipline of the communist parties, rather than in the mass appeal of their ideas.

Two of these revolutionary wars, however, had an immense impact reaching far beyond the normal bilateral imperial nexus. The first and longest was in Vietnam, whose war of independence stretched from the closing months of the Second World War through into the 1960s. In the process, it sparked a dramatic upsurge of political dissent in the West, connecting a new revolutionary generation to the struggles of the Third World. The second was in Cuba, where a small band of revolutionaries succeeded in overthrowing the US-dominated government in an astonishingly rapid (by the Maoist timescale of 'protracted war') rural guerrilla campaign between 1958 and 1961. A third conflict, the slow-burning struggle of the Palestinian Arabs to recover from and reverse the disaster of 1948, also played a key part in the rebirth of terrorism: here the turning point was the second 'disaster', the war of 1967, which placed the whole of Palestine under Israeli control.

Though terrorism was a significant element in both the Vietnam and Cuban wars, it was definitely subordinate to the logic of guerrilla warfare. In a systematic and ruthless campaign to eliminate collaboration, the Vietminh assassinated hundreds of village elders, together with anyone who cooperated with (or gave information to) the French authorities; altogether it and its successor the Vietcong may have killed 20,000 people in this way. For its part, Castro's rebel band, though minuscule in comparison with the Vietminh forces, likewise systematically 'executed' suspected informers – what Che Guevara called 'revolutionary justice' – to ensure its own survival. But this aspect of the Cuban experience was hardly foregrounded in the short handbook Che Guevara published in the euphoric period after Castro took power, *Guerrilla Warfare* (1961) – probably the most inspirational revolutionary tract of the century. A generation's attention was seized by Guevara's insistence that dedicated fighters could form a *'foco insurreccional'* which would generate a revolutionary situation. This stood orthodox Marxism on its head – a point hammered home in a more intellectual manner by Régis Debray (then a university teacher in Havana) in his equally celebrated *Revolution in the Revolution?* (1967) – and instantly threatened the old (in all senses) communist parties with irrelevance.

The Latin American link

The link between the Guevara–Debray theory of revolution and the return to terrorism may not seem obvious. But the next step followed almost naturally, as the Cuban revolutionary example resonated across Latin America. A leading example is the self-reinvention of the Brazilian communist leader Carlos Marighela, a Party stalwart until 1967 when he went to the Conference of the Organization for Latin American Solidarity in Havana, about the time Guevara himself was killed in his failed rural insurgency in Bolivia. In the brief period between founding the Revolutionary Communist Party in early 1968 and his death in a gunfight with Brazilian police in November 1969, Marighela embraced another inspirational concept, the 'urban guerrilla'. (Though the concept itself seems to have originated with a Spanish exile in Uruguay, Abraham Guillén, who had written the *Strategy of the Urban Guerrilla* in 1966.) Marighela's June 1969 *Minimanual of the Urban Guerrilla*, which reached a much wider audience, shifted the revolutionary focus back to the cities, but in a very different style from the tenets of classical Marxism.

Its opening sentence – 'Anyone who opposes the military dictatorship and wants to fight against it can do something, however little' – set its practical tone; and its treatment of terrorism (though surprisingly brief) reflected its opportunist spirit. Marighela first listed terrorism as one among 14 'methods of action', and defined it quite narrowly – 'By terrorism I mean the use of bomb attacks' – but immediately went on to include looting stocks of food for the benefit of the people. ('In the work of revolutionary terrorism the guerrilla must always be adaptable.') In an essay on 'Guerrilla Tactics', he made clear that 'terrorism alone will not win us power', but could 'demoralize the authorities'. 'Revolutionary terrorism's great weapon is initiative which guarantees its survival ... The more committed terrorists there are, the more military power will be worn down, the more fear and tension it will suffer....' But he insisted that terrorist acts were 'not designed to kill members of the common people, or to upset or intimidate them in any way'. Marighela was certainly not blind to the moral problems involved in all this, but he insisted that 'It is better to act mistakenly than do nothing for fear of doing wrong.' The ultimate guarantee could only be the moral superiority of the individual guerrilla, produced by the fact that he is 'defending a just cause, the cause of the people'.

Even then, the adoption of indiscriminate terror was still a little way off. The first serious efforts to take guerrilla warfare into the city, in Venezuela and Guatemala from 1963 to 1967, preserved the essential operating logic of rural guerrilla action. The Tactical Combat Units set up by the recently united Venezuelan Armed

Forces of National Liberation (FALN) in 1963 were each about a hundred strong (with supporting services in addition), though they divided more flexibly into 'shock units'. They briefly established 'liberated zones'. But they did not secure public support; indeed, their policy of assassinating policemen – all members of extended working-class Caracas families – had the opposite effect, and the Liberation Front suffered a serious defeat in the elections of 1964. In Guatemala, the quasi-Trotskyist Armed Rebel Forces led by Yon Sosa and Turcios Lima initially went in for what might be called armed education rather than propaganda by deed – they occupied villages and put on classes in socialist ideas – but in Guatemala City, their campaign consisted mainly of abduction and assassination, and degenerated into a sterile vendetta with security forces and vigilante counterterror groups.

Perhaps the most resonant of all Latin American urban guerrilla campaigns emerged in what was, in formal terms, the most democratic state south of the USA – Uruguay (once known as 'the Switzerland of America'), with one of the highest standards of living in Latin America. But Uruguay was in a prolonged economic crisis during the 1960s, with exports falling and inflation rising. The socialist-led insurgency followed the Guevarist model of starting from small beginnings. The Movement for National Liberation (MLN), universally known as the Tupamaros after the last independent Indian leader, Tupac Amaru (d. 1781), began operations in 1963 with a raid on a rifle club, and then spent a year preparing a cellular organization and studying the theory of Guillén. After that, they launched a series of operations designed to enrol public support, notably the revolutionary 'expropriations' and food distribution carried out by the 'hunger commando'. The climax of this campaign was the occupation of the town of Pando (25 kilometres outside Montevideo) in October 1969, a brilliant publicity stunt and 'homage to Che Guevara' on the second anniversary of his death. Less spectacular, and ultimately more problematic, was a series of kidnappings of US diplomats and businessmen, designed to focus attention on American imperialism (though they also held the British ambassador Geoffrey Jackson for eight months in 1971).

At this time, the Tupamaros seemed to be living the revolutionary dream: they had secured widespread public acceptance of their critique of the established order ('They're eaten up with pride and the worker can go hang', as one worker in Pando grated) and support for their operations. Not until 1972 did Uruguay's president declare a state of internal war, but after that the rapid shift to an increasingly authoritarian response – including the dissolution of parliament in June 1973 – successfully carried public opinion with it. Between 1971 and September 1972, the proportion of the public who thought the Tupamaros were pursuing social justice fell from 59% to 4%, despite the crumbling of the liberal constitution (press censorship and detention without trial were introduced) under pressure from the military – who ironically had discovered that some Tupamaro allegations of governmental corruption were true, and (as so often elsewhere) moved in to clean up the state administration. More vigorous 'antiterrorist' measures succeeded in breaking up an organization that had become more vulnerable; in its confidence that it could move on to open confrontation with the army, it had let its earlier tight security slip in favour of expansion. The end result was a far more illiberal state, and less social justice.

The verdict on urban guerrilla action was ultimately negative. A level-headed overall assessment of its benefits and costs, by the military analyst Anthony Burton in his 1975 book *Urban Terrorism*, is worth quoting:

> By huddling close to the enemy and the people, the former's superior firepower may be negated and the latter's revolutionary consciousness heightened. Central command and control is achieved and the articulation of political and military action, of strikes and demonstrations with armed attack, is made easier.

(We might add the high sensitivity of the government and the media to armed action in the capital city.) On the other hand,

> a city-centred strategy is unlikely by itself to succeed: the effort is difficult to sustain, problems of security and logistics become crucial, and the support of the people is likely to be lost if they are asked to hide and succour the terrorist over a long period with no apparent prospect of success against a patient and determined government.

A way of sidestepping that was to go underground, and finance the organization by 'expropriations', that is, bank robberies. Marighela had advocated these partly as tactical exercises for training and sustaining urban 'firing groups'; and it was the underground group that was to be the vehicle for the dramatic return of revolutionary terrorism to 'the West' in the late 1960s.

We believe that carrying out armed struggle will affect the people's consciousness of the nature of the struggle against the state. By beginning the armed struggle, the awareness of its necessity will be furthered. This is no less true in the US than in other countries throughout the world. Revolutionary action generates revolutionary consciousness; growing consciousness develops revolutionary action. Action teaches the lessons of fighting and demonstrates that armed struggle is possible.

Weather Underground, *Prairie Fire* (1974)

As early as 1970, the re-emergence of terrorism was plain enough for Ted Robert Gurr, a leading analyst of rebellion, to sketch the 'conventional wisdom' about terrorism amongst most officials and ordinary people in Western societies (and quite a few experts, he added) as a relatively new and particularly threatening form of political violence, resorted to especially by alienated, youthful members of the middle class, and increasing rapidly throughout the world. Gurr demonstrated that as generalizations, all these propositions were false; he noted, too, the irony of the fact that 'this particular fantasy of the revolutionary Left has been accepted as an ominous political reality by everyone else'. The data he used to map the characteristics of 'political terrorism in the 1960s' already showed 4,455 deaths resulting from terrorist campaigns and 167 from isolated terrorist 'episodes' between 1961 and 1970. Though of these only 245 deaths from campaigns and 26 deaths from isolated episodes were in Europe, as against 1,630/92 in Africa and Asia, and 2,580/48 in Latin America, he found that the totals of terrorist incidents and campaigns were greater in democratic than in autocratic political systems – 105 incidents, 72 campaigns in democratic countries, as compared to 21 incidents and 21 campaigns in autocratic ones – a finding he explained by postulating that 'terrorists *can* act with more impunity in quasi-open societies than in police states'. But he thought that terrorism was 'principally the tactic of groups that represent the interests and demands of small minorities' – not, in fact, revolutionary movements.

The wave of terrorist action was surprisingly widespread: even Britain witnessed the brief flurry of the loosely anarchist Angry Brigade (27 bombs and a number of bank robberies between 1968 and 1971), while the USA puzzled over the Weathermen – who aimed at 'forcing the disintegration of society' – and the inscrutable Symbionese Liberation Army – which vaulted to amazing celebrity by kidnapping and enrolling the publishing heiress Patty Hearst for a San Francisco bank robbery, but whose fight for 'oppressed minorities everywhere' was too diffuse to stike a chord with the public. Such causes emerged again in Belgium and France, where *Action Directe* set out as late as 1979 'to wreck society through direct action by destroying its institutions and the men who serve it', and later targeted 'the Americanization of Europe'. But the most troubling upsurges of terror were in Germany and, above all, Italy, where between 1969 and 1980 there were 12,690 incidents of terrorist violence, killing 362 people and wounding 4,524. These statistics suggested a real possibility of social breakdown in the most advanced societies.

Groupuscular terrorism

The 1970s seemed to be the age of the 'groupuscules', the tiny, fissiparous radical activist groups which spread across Western Europe. In Italy, no fewer than 597 terrorist groups (of both left and right) were counted, but one above all appeared to challenge and subvert most deeply held Western liberal assumptions, and pose most acutely the issue of terrorist motivation – the *Brigate Rosse* (BR; Red Brigades), formed in 1969. Their first violent actions, beginning with armed robberies ('proletarian expropriations') and the firebombing of cars and theatres, began in November 1970. The BR habitually signed their communiqués 'for communism'; their self-description was 'autonomous worker organizations that indicate the first moments of proletarian self-organization to fight the bosses and their henchmen with the same means that they use against the working class'. This suggested, however, at best an indirect relationship with the proletariat, and it seems clear that students played a major role in the adoption of violent methods. The by-now venerable tradition of Italian anarchism – and the example of neo-fascist terrorism also grimly in evidence during the 1960s – supplied the model. (A major early influence was the anarchist publisher Giangiacomo Feltrinelli, who died in a bomb misfire in 1972.) Student activism had been screwed up to an intense pitch by the virtual collapse of the university system, carrying a vast student population (over a million) and chronically underfunded. This crisis reflected the wider Italian social problem precipitated by an unsustainable shift of population from the countryside to the cities, and consequently spiralling unemployment.

The crisis of national confidence worsened through the 1970s under the impact of the 1973 oil supply crisis, while terrorist violence multiplied from 467 attacks in 1975 and 685 in

1976 through 1,806 in 1977 to 2,725 in 1978. The perceived effectiveness and legitimacy of the state continued to decline, and the number of Italians, particularly students, sympathetic to the terrorist movement was 'shockingly large'. The BR's emergence as the leading terrorist group during this period was confirmed when they mounted the spectacular kidnapping and eventual killing of Aldo Moro. Moro, a former and certain future prime minister, was a lynchpin of the fragile political system with its dependence on coalition-building. As a Christian Democrat (DC) leader, he figured in BR language as the 'godfather' of the 'imperialist counter-revolution organized by the DC'. He was thus a legitimate target at any time, but the timing of the abduction (in which his five bodyguards were killed in an operation so precisely executed that many people insisted it must be the work of foreigners; alternatively, low national self-esteem could be confirmed by pointing to the incompetence of Moro's security arrangements – no bullet-proof car, fixed daily routine) was determined by the approaching trial of key BR leaders in custody in Turin. At this stage, the Piedmontese capital, flooded with police and *carabinieri* who were still unable to prevent the BR from assassinating the chief of political police, came close to the ultimate terrorist scenario, 'dominated by fear, its people literally immobilized in a state of siege'.

The level of public discontent and the weakness of the state go some way to explaining the genuinely alarming impact of terrorism in Italy, but the case of Germany was plainly different. The upsurge of indiscriminate terror in the 1970s led by two small organizations – the communist 'Baader-Meinhof gang' (named the *Rote Armee Fraktion* [RAF], Red Army Group, as a gesture of respect for the 'Japanese Red Army group') and the anarchist June 2nd Movement (*Bewegung Zwei Juni*, or B2J, named after the day on which the police killed a student protester during the visit of the Shah of Iran) – needs still more careful explanation. The central link between the two countries was, of course, the historical legacy of fascism and Nazism, which drove a wedge between the

German postwar generation and their parents and made young people 'hypersensitive towards all authoritarian structures in society'. Instead, German youth culture turned towards America, and the resulting cocktail is etched on every page of the famous memoir written by 'Bommi' (Michael) Baumann in 1975 after he gave up his beloved bombs and left B2J – *Wie alles anfing*, translated into English as *Terror or Love?* (1979). For Baumann, bombs and Hare Krishna seem to have been equally enjoyable – even playful – ways of getting at the system.

How typical was Baumann? Unlike the leading thinkers and activists of the RAF, Ulrike Meinhof, Gudrun Ensslin, and Horst Mahler – or indeed Renato Curcio of the BR – he was not a middle-class student (he called them 'bookworms' and said he 'could never really get close to' their world). He preferred the less ideological counter-culture of 'commune K.1', a classic manifestation of sixties hippiedom. He had given up work in disgust at the sheer banality of everyday life – 'this mindless activity just to get your old age pension'. He was untypical, too, in not being recruited through a friendship network. (At least 843 out of 1,214 recruits to the much larger BR identified in one study already had a friend in the organization, and of these three-quarters had more than one, and nearly half had over seven.)

But Baumann's account crucially registers the catalytic impact of the collective experiences of 1968, the huge antagonism generated on the left by the tone – and dishonesty – of the right-wing press (witness Baumann's fury when Hanns-Martin Schleyer, a former Nazi, kidnapped and killed by the RAF in 1977, was portrayed by the press as an innocent victim), and the potent inspiration of foreign guerrilla/terrorist movements. In the chaper entitled 'Tupamaros West Berlin', we witness the dramatic militarization of his group after a visit to the Popular Front for the Liberation of Palestine (PFLP) training camp in Lebanon. He also vividly conveys the sheer excitement of armed action. As his nickname suggests, he became fascinated by the use of explosives, and the closest studies made of these clandestine organizations underline the role of the continuous presence of weapons in the daily life of the group. This 'very special relationship with guns' was part of the distinctiveness which bound individuals to their comrades. The totality of individuals' commitment to the group's aims, and the binding effect of their detachment from normal life, have been repeatedly identified as the key dynamics of these very small organizations, which became effectively Burkean 'little platoons' (though they preferred unit names like 'cadre' or 'commando'). As Susan Stern of the Weathermen recalled, 'We were alone and isolated . . . Ignoring the reality, we filled our minds with visions of the new underground.' Together they were 'contra mundum', and as their isolation from the public made it increasingly difficult for them to see their actions as political successes, they turned more completely to acceptance of military evaluation, envisaging their campaign in terms of 'war'. Repression often accelerated recruitment, as it did after the Moro incident, and the death of terrorist 'martyrs' in prison – Holger Meins and Ulrike Meinhof in 1976; Baader, Ensslin, and Raspe in 1977.

But all this still left a dizzying gap between the limited military means available and the ambitious aims of these groups. A constant mantra in 'Euroterrorist' literature was 'Never be deterred by the enormous dimensions of your own goals' (as the French group *Action Directe* told itself). Their targeting policy moved towards increasingly destructive and indiscriminate action for two distinct reasons. First, this shift fits the fundamental logic of the clandestine groups' existence: that the moral values of the normal world were part of the system that had to be overthrown. Second, it ups the stakes, in effect exchanging the propaganda value of justification for greater shock value, and ensuring massive media coverage. Such publicity can disguise the absence of any corresponding shift in public opinion. Detachment from the real world may also, as the German philosopher Jurgen Habermas disapprovingly said, be heightened by other elements of 'youth culture': 'culture transmitted through electronic gadgetry never

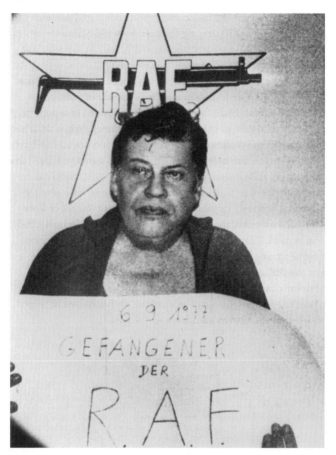

8. Hanns-Martin Schleyer, the industrialist (and former SS man) taken hostage by the *Rote Armee Fraktion* (RAF) in April 1977, a bid to secure the release of the group's leaders Andreas Baader and Gudrun Ensslin from prison – the placard reads 'prisoner of the RAF'

quite loses its game character and superficiality, and contains the inherent danger of portraying the pseudo-world of entertainment as reality'.

So we may conclude that Western revolutionary terrorist groups have relied on pure terrorism mainly as a result of political weakness or marginality – even perhaps solipsism. In a political sense, then, the threat they have posed is minimal. When detached from the wider revolutionary movement, as Guevara and Debray pointed out, terrorism is self-defeating. The destructive tally of the RAF by the time it sank into inaction in the 1980s, for instance, was statistically as small as the group's size might have predicted. Statistics, however, cannot convey the corrosive impact of their campaign on public morale and civic confidence in Germany, Italy, and beyond. They demonstrated that however resilient societies may be in objective terms, they remain psychologically fragile. For the Italian journalist Luigi Bonante, writing in 1978, 'contemporary terrorism wounds that which seems to us to be one of the few judgments of value we all find ourselves in accord with – that the democratic system is the best'.

Chapter 5
Nationalism and terror

> Men must be aroused, pushed, shocked by the very benefits
> of their own deliverance, their eyes wounded with the
> truth, light thrown in terrible handfuls.
>
> P. J. P. Tynan, *The Irish National Invincibles* (1894)

The level of shock administered to Western establishments by small-group terrorism was registered in the level of attention lavished on it. The torrent of analysis had by the 1980s created a severely distorted perspective. The persistence of the model of the individual terrorist as an alienated Western youth was remarkable: its reductive effect obscured the deeper and more varied impulses to terrorist action which, as the cultural historian Khachig Tololyan insisted, can only be grasped by cultural interpretation. We need to understand 'the way in which different societies maintain their vision of their collective selves, and so produce different terrorisms and different terrorists'. In other words, the framework for much modern terrorist action is ethnic or nationalist; and each nationalism is culturally unique. Indeed, the emblematic terrorist act of the early 20th century – the assassination of Archduke Franz Ferdinand, heir to the throne of Austria-Hungary, at Sarajevo in June 1914 – was carried out by a Serbian nationalist. The vast bulk of subsequent terrorism (whether on governmental criteria or by the more selective standards applied here) was similarly the work of nationalists.

Nationalist movements have shown much greater resilience – not to mention destructive capacity – than the small and fissiparous left-wing revolutionary groups. They tend to be significantly bigger, for one thing, and to draw on a broader pool of recruitment; and though their 'cause' – freeing or uniting the nation – is not necessarily more practicable than the revolutionary dream of total social transformation, nationalism has dominated modern politics precisely because it connects with a visceral, apparently natural force. (In fact, the principle of national self-determination, the idea that nations should possess political sovereignty in order to realize their cultural distinctness, is an intellectual invention of the 19th century.) Thus even a nation whose struggle seems objectively doomed to failure (say the Chechens, or indeed the Irish as defined by the republican movement) may never give up; while an ethnic group such as the Tamil Tigers (Liberation Tigers of Tamil Eelam, LTTE) reached stratospheric levels of deadliness – well over 100,000 were killed by them in their 33-year career.

Tololyan's own example, the Armenians, provide a potent illustration – 'a deadly and important manifestation of international terrorism'. Modern Armenian terrorism dates from 1890 (a vital epoch in the national revival throughout Europe), when the 'Dashnags' (*Hye Heghapkhaganneri Dashnagtzootyun*; Federation of Armenian Revolutionaries) were organized in imitation of the *Narodniki*. But their actions, like those of subsequent Armenian groups – most famously the attempted seizure of the Turkish Embassy in Lisbon by the Armenian Revolutionary Army (ARA) in 1983 – were shaped by a long historical memory reaching back to the legendary struggle of Vartan against the Persians c. AD 450. This was a religious rather than a 'national' defence, but it has become incorporated with later struggles, above all the massacres of the 1890s and 'the genocide' of

1916, into what Tololyan calls a 'typological-prefigurative narrative' – a story of the people in which historical changes of context are elided: past and future become one whole. Where the nation is without a state, the task of preserving cultural identity is at its most demanding, and the requirement of action most pressing. 'We know what must be done.'

In the nationalist worldview, the rights of all nations are equal, whatever their size, location, or practical viability. The prime issue is one of consciousness: whether the members of the nation itself are convinced of their collective identity as envisaged by the nationalists. (Witness the Armenian nationalist anxiety about assimilation, which they call 'white massacre', or Irish nationalist reaction against 'Anglicization'.) Lack of national consciousness is seen as evidence of the cultural peril they must fight. Terrorism may play a leading part in the attempt to preserve or 'reawaken' the national spirit, and also in the accompanying (or maybe resulting) struggle against a foreign or imperial government. But there is another and possibly more intractable problem: what all too often stands in the way of national liberation movements is not only the foreign government, but the fact that people of other ethnic groups live within the presumed national territory. (It seems to be the junction of socially constructed unity – culture – with occupation of land that persuades people that the nation is a natural, or even divinely ordained, unit; but it is seldom a neat one.) These other groups may resist incorporation within the insurgent nation. In this case, another dimension of terrorism may appear; the communal slaughter which has now come to be called by the (nationalist) euphemism 'ethnic cleansing'. Even if they do not resist, the result may be the same. Nationalists are intolerant of diversity or plurality; as an unkind critic puts it, 'nationalism is driven by a bovine will to simplify things'.

Once rooted, nationalist 'causes' are hardly ever given up – in modern times, despite predictions that the world is moving into a post-national age, they look virtually indestructible. A number of nationalist groups have maintained terrorist campaigns for a generation or more, and to grasp the reasons for this we need, even more than in the case of revolutionary terror, to know their history.

The case of Irish republicanism

The longest-lived of them, so far, is the Irish republican movement, whose most recent armed campaign has lasted 30 years at the time of writing, and which can confidently trace its ancestry back another half-century at least. And though tactics have varied over time, the Irish Republican Army (IRA), whether Official, Provisional, Continuity, or Real, still follows the operating logic laid down by the Irish Revolutionary Brotherhood in the 1850s. In terms of organization and method, the continuity may be thought to stretch yet further back, into the agrarian terrorism of the Catholic 'Defenders' of the 18th century. (Though whether these represented the Irish nation is still a sensitive political point.) It is worth pondering the reasons for this almost unblinking commitment to the use of political violence.

The original 'physical force' group, the Irish Revolutionary Brotherhood (IRB; colloquially known as the Fenians; 'the Organization' to its members) began life around 1858 as a classical insurrectionist group, believing in the capacity of a small armed vanguard to energize and lead the people in open rebellion. It faced two primary difficulties: first, organizing in secret to avoid police surveillance; and second, choosing the critical moment to raise the flag of revolt. The imperative of security impelled them to follow the organizational pattern of continental Freemasonry, with a sequence of carefully controlled levels of initiation. This, ironically, made them look like the oathbound agrarian secret societies like 'Captain Moonlight' which fought for control of the land in Ireland, a struggle which the Fenians themselves rejected as debasing the cause of national independence. Oathbound secrecy also led them to fall foul of the Catholic Church, which condemned them as free-thinking subversives. Their biggest problem, though, was that a secret organization could do little to prepare the people for the insurrectionary moment. It had to hope that (what it believed to be) the innate popular desire for national independence would be enough to spread the spark of armed action to send the masses up against the guns of the government. This did not happen – in Ireland, in Italy, or anywhere else that insurrectionist groups patiently organized and waited.

The republican shift to terrorism, which might be thought inevitable from a 20th-century perspective, was surprisingly hesitant and contested. The failure of 'military' Fenianism – the apparently promising idea of infiltrating the Irish regiments of the British Army to turn their rank and file against Britain – in 1864–6 was followed by a 'spectacular' action, the 1867 Clerkenwell explosion, which may be seen as the world's first urban bombing. But it was accidental, and was not repeated. The leadership of the Fenian organization in Ireland remained committed to the concept of 'honourable warfare' and hostile to terrorism, which they associated with the murky activities of the agrarian secret societies. Yet the Clerkenwell explosion had a far bigger impact on British politics than any of the IRB's 'honourable' military efforts. It can certainly be credited with two major reforms, launched by Gladstone in 1868 under the banner of 'pacifying Ireland'. The IRB Supreme Council was unmoved by these achievements, which it judged irrelevant, or even damaging, to the struggle for national liberation.

Other Irish republicans were certainly less fastidious. Both O'Donovan Rossa's Skirmishers and the Irish-American Clan na Gael adopted frankly terrorist methods in the 1880s, the latter clearly influenced by anarchist and populist action. Rossa (who stuck to gunpowder) seemed to accept that even if he could do no more than 'hurt England' that would be enough. But the Clan went for the full dynamite effect. Yet its explosions in London, though bigger than in 1867, proved to have less effect – mainly, in an early illustration of a classic pattern, they initiated the erosion of traditional English freedoms, notably via the creation of Britain's first political police, the Irish Special Branch. Later revolutionary terrorist strategists would see this process as part of a radicalization of the struggle, but for the Irish republicans, the British failed to overreact sufficiently. This unpredictability of reaction represents a central weakness in the terror process.

> Such a strategy relies on the premise that the British people do not support British government sponsored murder in Ireland, that they want their troops withdrawn from Ireland, as indicated in opinion polls, and that they have the potential to eventually force the British government because of the cost of the war or the attrition rate or because of the demoralisation and war weariness, to withdraw from Ireland.
>
> Provisional IRA statement, *An Phoblacht/Republican News*, 5 January 1984

By contrast with the Clan's embrace of the new technology of high explosives, the most resonant of all the Irish 'terrorist' actions of this time, the 1882 Phoenix Park assassinations of the two leading members of the Irish government, was carried out with surgical knives. (Helping to ensure, amongst other things, that in future ministers would seldom be allowed to walk about unguarded.) By contrast, too, the political message of this act was hard to decipher, since the 'Irish National Invincibles' never carried out another, or issued any political manifesto. If the killing of Gladstone's son-in-law pushed him towards Home Rule, was this what the Invincibles wanted?

The failure of the Clan dynamite campaign brought direct Irish–American violent action in Britain to a surprisingly complete end, in contrast with the extraordinary resilience of the 'physical force' movement in Ireland itself. (They deployed the potent symbol of the 'phoenix flame' which would rekindle from its own ashes.) Its apparent decay around the turn of the century, so marked that almost everybody wrote it off, in fact coincided with a major reinvigoration, and refocusing, of Irish cultural identity in the form of the Gaelic revival. The dramatic insurrection in Dublin in 1916 represented a fusion of the old organization with the explicitly ethnic objectives formulated by Patrick Pearse – 'Ireland not free merely, but Gaelic also'. In Pearse's writing, the 'resonating roll-call that blurs history, context and nuance', which Tololyan identifies as the core of national ideology, is startlingly vivid. His call to violent action, too, was suffused with the ideal of 'death knowingly grasped' so central to the Armenian Vartan story – as, indeed, was the martyrdom of hunger-striking republican prisoners after the failure of the rising, most famously Thomas Ashe in 1917 and Terence MacSwiney in 1920.

Though Irish republicanism's commitment to physical force was consistent, its ambivalence about terrorist methods was partly due to the imprecision of its thinking about the utility of violence as such. Was the point of violent action simply to 'hurt England' – in the hope presumably that Britain would eventually get fed up and quit – or could it directly drive out the enemy? Given the huge disparity in available force, the second idea was almost literally suicidal. But it seems to have been what motivated most 'physical force men'. Research into the IRA's mainland campaign, for instance, has shown little in the way of reasoning about the effect of 'operations abroad', beyond the need to find 'something to do' and the urge to 'do to you what you are doing to Ireland', as one of the Manchester arsonists of April 1921 put it. Wild terrorist projects were framed by Cathal Brugha, but Michael Collins, using a more realistic test of their utility, repeatedly interfered to shut them down.

By contrast, the effectiveness of terrorism against 'spies and informers' was a pivotal factor in sustaining the republican guerrilla campaign in the Irish countryside, where the old grammar of agrarian intimidation was absorbed into the new logic of nationalism. Most crucially, IRA violence provoked a British counterterror that severely damaged the remaining legitimacy of the government. The 'Black and Tans', a semi-military temporary force recruited in Britain, became a byword for how-not-to combat a modern insurgency. Even though they were quite successful in persuading the Irish public to distance themselves from IRA activity, their methods raised a storm of public criticism. By 1921, the IRA could claim to have withstood the worst that the British Empire could throw at it; its survival became a beacon of hope to nationalist resistance movements all over the world. Yet by its own criteria republicanism had failed. After the split and the Civil War of 1922–3, the IRA opted out of politics, and launched two unequivocally terrorist campaigns: the 'mainland' bombing campaign of 1938–9, and the border campaign of 1956–62; both petered out without causing much stir. By the mid-1960s, the 'physical force' idea was probably more marginalized than at any time in its history; the dramatic revival of terrorist action in the 1970s would have been impossible to predict. It followed the chaotic breakdown of the dominant Unionist group in Northern Ireland in face of demands for reform. The Provisional IRA emerged as a communal defence force in 1970 and can plausibly be portrayed as a national liberation front with a sideline in terrorist action, rather than as a terrorist organization. A handful of 'spectaculars' have been accompanied by a stream of street-level killings that are effectively sectarian and represent an ongoing vendetta between republican and loyalist paramilitary groups, rather than a serious attempt to influence public opinion.

Its organizational resilience has remained remarkable, for various reasons: crucially, the number of volunteers required for active service at any time is in the low hundreds, and recruitment has never been difficult because of the organization's established reputation in the nationalist community. Its self-image as a people's army (in the nationalist not Maoist sense, though the blurring has sometimes been encouraged) has survived replacement of traditional military structure by cellular organization from the late 1970s onwards. (As the IRA Army Council's 'Green Book' declares, 'Commitment to the Army is total belief in the Army...that the Army is the direct representative of the 1918 Dail.') Its self-belief is fuelled by potent historical legend, and reinforced by contemporary successes, producing a robust faith in the cause: both its abstract justice and its pragmatic feasibility (despite long-term evidence to the contrary); backed by a belief that the essential unity and fraternity of the Irish people (including many who apparently repudiate this allegiance) is only fractured by deliberate British interference. As one investigator found, 'relatively few individuals offer sophisticated political justifications of violence, yet all show a strength of what can only be described as a belief in the rightness of their actions'.

Bringing such an organization back into the realm of politics is a complicated business. Though the British government proclaimed this as its objective (abjuring republicans to renounce violence), its policies had the opposite effect. It made a determined effort to pin

9. **The bomb placed in Enniskillen by the IRA on 8 November 1987 was deliberately aimed at a key symbol of Unionist identity, a Remembrance Day parade: 11 were killed and 63 injured**

the 'terrorist' label on the Provisional IRA through the policy of 'criminalization' in the late 1970s, starting with the withdrawal of the political status given to republican internees. (Admittedly, the idea of 'political status' had always been dubious in British law – a point Mrs Thatcher relentlessly proclaimed with her mantra 'crime is crime is crime' – but the decision to make an issue of this was significant.) The IRA's response, the hunger strike campaign, equally proclaimed its determination to assert its belligerent status. Though some analysis have been prepared to classify hunger strikes as terrorist actions, public perceptions of self-sacrifice have been more ambivalent (perhaps awe, tinged with admiration, rather than fear), and the outcome of the struggle was a moral defeat for the government which paved the way for the cautious re-entry of the physical force leadership into politics, whose outcome still hangs in the balance.

Violence or politics: the case of ETA

An ambivalent relationship with politics has also characterized the stance of the most persistent of the other ethnic terrorist organizations in Europe over the last generation, the Basque separatist *Euzkadi to Askatasuna* (ETA; Land and Freedom). Created in 1959, but drawing like the IRA on a long-established cultural resistance movement (and also a strong Catholic ethos), ETA defined itself as a movement of national liberation and not a political party. It engaged rather more openly with the question of Basque national identity itself than did the IRA with that of 'Irishness' (an issue the IRA was reluctant to highlight). The Basque country had, like Ireland but for different reasons, been flooded with migrants (from Spain), drawn by its rapid economic development in the 19th century. ETA departed from earlier racial theories and also rejected any religious dimension by advocating strict secularism: the objective was to assimilate anyone who was prepared to use the Basque language. (This line was initiated in Ireland also by the Gaelic language movement at the end of the 19th century, but by that time the Irish people themselves had abandoned the language and have not subsequently been persuaded to readopt it.)

ETA is rhetorically at least a socialist revolutionary as well as a nationalist movement, but though it has often levied 'revolutionary taxation' at gunpoint, its attacks have mostly been directed at representatives of the Spanish state rather than the often-denounced industrial capitalists. Though it is no more prepared than any contemporary organization to accept the label terrorist, the carefully controlled tempo of its campaign and the symbolic nature of its selected targets have distanced it from even the Provisional IRA's approximation of a guerrilla insurgency. In the period from the start of the military campaign in June 1968 to the end of 1980 (analysed by Robert Clark, 1984), it killed 287 people and injured about 400. Significantly, very few of these casualties were inflicted under the Franco regime: the ETA campaign accelerated after the election of the first democratic assembly in 1977, and peaked with the granting of autonomy and the election of the Basque assembly in 1980 – it killed nearly 100 people in that year. Its use of indiscriminate attacks remained sparing (though, as in the bombing of Madrid airport and railway stations in July 1979, still very shocking). Overall, its targeting was focused primarily on the Guardia Civil and the police. It showed a marked preference for the use of comparatively accurate weapons – small arms rather than explosives – and a determination repeatedly to attack high-ranking officials and officers, the highest being Admiral Carrero Blanco in 1973, and others, including the military governors of Madrid and Guipúzcoa in 1979. But it also achieved a big shock effect by kidnapping an obscure local councillor of the governing Partido Popolar in July 1997, and killing him when the government refused its demand to relocate ETA prisoners to the Basque country.

What has it achieved? The killing of Carrero Blanco, one of the most spectacular of all assassinations, in which the prime minister's car was blown 70 feet in the air by a mine, may have

10. ETA representatives seated in front of an ETA flag, 22 March 2006

brought the Francoist system to an end. But ETA was no more kindly disposed to the Spanish democracy that followed it. Its campaign has the hallmarks of 'classical' terrorism, operating at a tangent to politics on the assumption that it can connect with deeper realities. ETA has rejected concessions that have gone far beyond the reforms that the *Narodniki* said they would accept, and that the Provisional IRA may now have accepted. (Or at least the military section, ETAm, has done so; the 'political-military', ETApm, has largely accepted constitutionalism and many of its members took up the official amnesty, being allowed to 're-enter' society on condition they forswore violence.) As in Ireland, there is a deep rift between nationalists who can accommodate to a kind of autonomy and those who hold to the purist separatist ideal. As one of ETA's young women leaders put it, 'if we don't fight, the

Basques will perish as a people'. The attractive power of the ideal still burns brightly, above all for Basque youth.

ETA sometimes acknowledged mistakes, as when it apologized after bombing a Madrid supermarket in 1987. But its ferocity was as daunting as its internal discipline. Like the IRA it declared a number of truces and ceasefires during its fifty-year campaign of violence. These were not taken seriously enough to allow any progress to political negotiations, and it was widely seen as irredeemably militarist. The Spanish state's deep hostility to armed separatism was demonstrated in the government's attempt, without any evidence at all, to pin the 2004 Madrid train bombings on ETA. In March 2006, and again in September 2010, it declared ceasefires, the last of these being declared 'permanent' in January 2011. (Sinn Fein under Gerry Adams claimed to have helped persuade the movement to return to politics.)

ETA was unusual amongst nationalists in studiously avoiding targeting other ethnic groups – something the IRA certainly fails to do (while protesting that it does: Protestants are allegedly attacked not *qua* Protestants, or foreigners, but as security force members or helpers – implausible in the bombings at Enniskillen, or Omagh). The IRA are the more typical in this. The logic of national liberation, however liberal its rhetoric, requires a coherent national community which is necessarily defined in contrast with outsiders. Protecting this exclusivity is indeed the essence of nationalism. (Even though there have been socialist revolutionaries, like Connolly, who thought that national liberation was the first step towards international brotherhood, they have all been disappointed.) So the possibility that violence will be turned not only against the oppressor state but also against other ethnic groups is implicit.

Ethnic terror has shown little sign of dying out in the 20th century – if anything the reverse. In Belfast, for instance, the

communal violence unleashed in July 1920 lasted on and off
for two years, and killed more people than had died in all the
many riots of the 19th century put together. Thousands of
Catholic – 'Nationalist' – families were driven from their homes by
arson and assault, as the Protestant majority tidied up the
borders of its neighbourhoods. The same thing was repeated on a
still more extended timescale after 1968; and even as the 'peace
process' appeared to be taking firm root around the millennium
a ferocious territorial struggle broke out over the access of
Catholic children to a primary school in Ardoyne. Was this
terrorism or, as some might say, just general terror? The violence is
indirect and intimidatory as much as coercive, certainly,
although its intent is not to convert but to drive out those who
identify with the victims. But there is little sign of deliberate
planning or organization. Perhaps here language reaches its useful
limits; where fear and suspicion are so deeply entrenched, there
is no need or even possibility of strategic thinking: action is
reflexive and visceral. (Obedient, almost, to Bismarck's deadly
injunction, 'Germans! Think with your blood!')

Zionism and the problem of territory

The potential of nationalism to generate double-edged terrorism is
starkly demonstrated in the history of Zionism in Palestine. The
Zionist idea, the 'return' of the Jewish diaspora to Eretz Israel,
incorporated both the central objectives of modern nationalism:
the spiritual self-realization of the 'cultural' nation, and its physical
security against external threats. (Security in particular was, for
Jews in Eastern Europe, always under threat.) When Britain
committed itself through the 1917 Balfour Declaration to 'the
establishment in Palestine of a national home for the Jewish
people', it did not grasp either the full implications of these
objectives, or the difficulty of fulfilling them in face of Arab
resistance. Jewish security could be achieved in either of two ways:
by befriending the Arab population or by neutralizing, if not
removing it. A minority of Zionists (notably the tiny Brit Shalom

group) pursued the first course; another minority (the 'Revisionists' led by Vladimir Jabotinsky) insisted that Jews must be prepared to fight for statehood. The majority simply hoped for the best.

The international Zionist Organization and the majority of the *Yishuv* (the Jewish community living in Palestine at that time) were committed to reliance on Britain, but even they immediately set about establishing a semi-open defensive force (*Haganah*) in response to the first Arab attacks on Jewish settlements in 1920. The repetition of those attacks in 1921 and, more violently, in 1929 were a terrible trauma for moderate Zionists: the movement really faced the option of abandoning the entire project of building a 'national home' in Palestine or accepting that it could only be done by force. The majority was eventually brought to accept this by Britain's ungenerous policy during the Holocaust, but the Revisionists were already prepared for a showdown long before the Jewish community had even reached one-third of Palestine's population. There would certainly have been a significant Jewish terrorist campaign during the Arab rebellion of 1936–9 but for the fact that Arab violence was primarily directed at the British authorities; the terrorism that appeared was mainly action by the Arab guerrilla fighters, or *mujahideen*, against their rivals for leadership of the Palestinian Arab people – internal enforcement terror.

Jewish terrorist action took off towards the end of World War II with the assassination in Cairo in 1944 of Lord Moyne by the 'Stern Gang', an outgrowth of the Revisionist movement. But though the campaigns of the Irgun Zvai Leumi (IZL) and Lehi (Lohamei Heruth Israel; Freedom Fighters for Israel, or FFI) are routinely labelled terrorist – and indeed they are presented as textbook examples of the efficacy of terrorism in certain circumstances – we need to register that, apart from a small number of spectacular operations – the bombing of the King David Hotel in Jerusalem in July 1946 being the most deadly terrorist attack so far – their targeting was precise and mainly military. (The King David itself housed British military headquarters, though most of the casualties were local civilians.) The British Army did not like describing its Jewish opponents as terrorists – though the government insisted on doing so – because of the implication that its troops were frightened by them. Before its first and most famous operation the assassination of Lord Moyne in 1944, Lehi accepted the term as it had been used by the Russian Populists, and maintained that 'terror is, for us, part of contemporary political warfare'. But it was realistic about its limits: in 1943 its publicity sheet *Hechazit* declared,

> If the question is, is it possible to bring about liberation by means of terror? the answer is: No! If the question is, do these actions help to bring liberation nearer? the answer is: Yes!

It also explained its function:

> It is not aimed at persons, but at representatives and is therefore effective. And if it also shakes the population out of its complacency, so much the better.

In fact, it proved to deliver much more than this cautious estimate. The fact that Moyne himself, a former colonial secretary who had presided over Britain's policy of excluding Jewish refugees from Palestine (and so was certainly seen as a legitimate target), was a friend of Winston Churchill, probably the only remaining pro-Zionist British senior politician, magnified the effect of his killing. While Churchill abandoned plans to partition Palestine and create a Jewish state, issuing doom-laden warnings about the termination of the Zionist dream 'in the smoke of assassins' pistols', Revisionists had long since written off British friendship as useless. Their violent campaign played a central part in bringing the majority of the *Yishuv* around to their view. Here the classic terrorist argument that government repression would drive the people on to the side of the terrorists was borne out. (As, too, in

Ireland in 1920–1.) The British proved unexpectedly incompetent and irresolute repressors, quickly demoralized by the energy and ruthlessness of the Jewish campaign. When they abandoned Palestine in 1948 they did so in a way that created the maximum chaos – a situation the terrorists were ideally positioned to exploit.

The difficulty of writing objectively about terrorism is starkly illustrated by the fact that even those studies that provide a clear and critical account of the Jewish terrorist campaign stop dead at the point of the British decision to withdraw from Palestine. (Loaded works such as those by Netanyahu, so prominent in the published literature, don't mention Jewish terrorism at all; for them terrorism in Palestine is exclusively Arab.) Yet the subsequent campaign of the Palestine Liberation Organization

11. The destruction of the south wing of the King David Hotel in Jerusalem by the Irgun on 22 July 1946 killed 91 people, mostly civilian employees of the British government and military authorities in Palestine

(PLO) is quite literally incomprehensible without an understanding of the grim aftermath in which the Jewish state substantially enlarged its share (allotted by a United Nations Special Commission) of Palestine's land area and the Palestine Arab state collapsed. Most writers put this struggle in the category of war – international rather than civil. This reflects the Israeli state's foundation myth, that it was attacked by an overwhelming combination of Arab states. In this life-and-death struggle, the Arab inhabitants of Palestine became legitimate targets. And while there was indeed a military reason for occupying such villages as Deir Yassin, there was none for the massacre of their inhabitants (who were known to be non-resistant), save the belief that every Arab was a threat. If this was indeed war, these were war crimes. But they were more than that; they were a system. The Deir Yassin attack was carried out by members of the Irgun and Lehi, disavowed by the official Zionist leaders; but after the incorporation of the former terrorists ('dissidents' in official language) with the *Haganah* and *Palmach* into a new Israeli army, the violent clearance of Arab communities continued. (One expellee was the Christian George Habash of Lydda, later to lead the PFLP.) The transmission of terror produced a growing tide of refugees, the permanent victims of *al-Nakbah*, the 'disaster'.

Can terror liberate nations?

Jewish terrorism proved stronger than both its key opponents. But this outcome was rare indeed. By contrast, the campaigns of the Palestine Liberation Organization, and the more radical Popular Front for the Liberation of Palestine (PFLP), have been much longer than those of the Irgun and Lehi, but far less successful. Indeed, they could in one sense be argued to have been counterproductive: the general position of the Arabs of Palestine is dramatically worse than it was at the outset of the 'international' terrorist campaign in 1969. [As against that, there has been a symbolic gain, the establishment of the PLO-controlled administration for Gaza and Jericho.] Beyond doubt, the use of high-profile terrorism in the 1970s brought the Palestinian case to world attention in a way that two decades of suffering in comparative silence had not.

In fact, terrorist action had been initiated by Palestinian refugees since the early 1950s, but the main result had been the provocation of major Israeli military action – ultimately the two crushing wars of 1956 and 1967. And, as George Habash of the PFLP said, the world ignored them. The effect of the PFLP's hijacking of an El Al airliner on 22 July 1968 was radically different. 'When we hijack a plane it has more effect than if we killed a hundred Israelis in battle', as Habash exulted in 1970 'the world is talking about us now'. The talk became deafening after what may be regarded as the emblematic terrorist action of the later 20th century, the seizure of Israeli athletes at the Munich Olympics in 1972. The international reaction was far-reaching: on the one hand the recognition of the PLO as a kind of virtual government-in-exile, and on the other the proliferation of expensive, burdensome, and possibly dangerous security measures (see Chapter 7). But its impact on the policy of Israel, which has responded (consistently with Revisionist thinking) with disproportionate and fairly approximate 'retaliation', and steady persistence in the colonization of the territories occupied in 1967, is less clear.

So the undoubted success of Zionist terrorism in creating a Jewish state was qualified in the longer term by a legacy of violence, generated (as in Ireland) by partition. Partition was also the outcome of the almost-successful campaign of EOKA in Cyprus in the 1950s. The organization's title – Ethniki Organosis Kyprion Agoniston – besides demonstrating the merging of ethnic and national, indicated its lack of appeal to the Turkish population of the island. Despite the clinical efficiency of its guerrilla terrorist campaign in undermining British power, it failed to achieve its declared political aim of *enosis*

12. One of the most characteristic actions in the Palestinian conflict: 22 ordinary Israelis were killed when this bus was bombed by Hamas in Jerusalem in February 1996

(union with Greece) or its fundamental – if unspoken – aim of liberating the whole island.

The effectiveness of terrorism in achieving national liberation also appeared to be demonstrated in the Algerian war of independence. The *Front de Libération nationale* (FLN; National Liberation Front) lauched its rebellion in 1954 but was making little progress until it adopted in 1966 the terrorist logic advocated by Ramdane Abane. Abane urged that a single killing in Algiers – where the US press would report it – was more effective than ten in the remote countryside, and he insisted that the morality of terrorism simply paralleled that of government repression: 'I see little difference between the girl who places a bomb in the Milk-Bar and the aviator who bombs a village or drops napalm in a *zone interdite*.'

The most careful assessment of FLN terror in Algeria has concluded that terrorism 'was integral to the revolution'. 'It served major political objectives' – securing the FLN's popular credibility and its internal cohesion, damaging the colonial regime, and enhancing the FLN's 'image of strength and determination abroad'. But for all its high profile, FLN terrorism was part of a wider campaign, including rural guerrilla warfare, nonviolent methods, and the establishment of a counter-government 'that was more effective than the French administration'. (A significant parallel with the Irish republican campaign of 1919–21.) Terrorism was particularly effective in launching the insurgency, but it went on being used when it was not necessary or functional. This does seem to indicate the danger that a kind of organizational habit of terror, with its low costs and scattergun effects, may become ingrained. And where that happens, the price of freedom may be higher than it first appears: it may have, as the jurist Richard Falk suggests, 'corrupting consequences that reverberate for decades'. At the end of the 20th century, the Algerian government was facing the eighth year of a 'terrorist' campaign mounted by the Armed Islamic Group (GIA) and the Salafi Group for Call and Combat (GSPC). According to official figures, this had killed no fewer than 100,000 people.

What this means in human terms may be hinted at by this extract from the diary of a Kabyle schoolteacher in the midst of the FLN campaign of the 1950s:

Toward noon I made a rapid tour of the town. People seem tense, ready for any madness, any anger, any stupidity. I felt through the crowd an impression of horror, as though I were living in the midst of a nightmare. An indefinable curse reigns over us.... At each execution of a traitor, or pretended such, anguish seizes the survivors. Nobody is sure of anything, it is truly terror. Terror of

the soldier, terror of the outlaw. Each of us is guilty just because
he belongs to such a category, such a race, such a people. You
fear they will make you pay with your life for your place in the world
or the colour of your skin. . . . you wonder why you don´t do
anything – even sincerely mourn the victims, mourn them in the
shadow of that secret and inadmissible joy which is that
of the escapee.

Chapter 6
Religious terror

> To fight in defence of religion and belief is a collective duty;
> there is no other duty after belief than fighting the enemy
> who is corrupting our life and our religion.
>
> Ibn Taymiyya, c. 1300

At the end of the 20th century, the world faced a revival of religious
fundamentalism, a puzzling development to many who had
assumed that the process of secularization was, however uneven,
an irreversible one. The long-standing liberal assumption that the
rise of modern society and the demise of religion were two sides of
the same coin was suddenly thrown into doubt; and the shock
effect of this was soon registered in writing on terrorism, where
religion had been confidently consigned to the margins of terrorist
motivation. The leading early studies, such as Walter Laqueur's in
1977 or Grant Wardlaw's a decade later, were determinedly
political. (Wardlaw deliberately entitled his book *Political
Terrorism*: it is interesting that he did not mention religious
motivation even to exclude it – as he did terror for 'criminal or
personal ends' – from the scope of his study.)

In the 1980s, terrorism was still the business of a handful of
radical revolutionaries and some all-too-familiar nationalists.
The next ten years, however, saw a remarkable shift. One of the

leading surveys in the late 1990s asserted that 'the religious imperative for terrorism is the most important defining characteristic of terrorism today', while the author of an American college textbook on terrorism put 'religious fanaticism' top of her list of terrorist motives. Official assessments reflect this too; for instance, the *Canadian Security Intelligence Service 2000 Public Report* stated that 'one of the prime motivators of contemporary terrorism is Islamic religious extremism'. Ten years later, 'the threat from Islamist extremism' remained the 'priority concern'. And while the US State Department remains unshakably regional-political in orientation, and still does not isolate religion as a category in its statistical breakdown – though it hangs determinedly on to international 'state-sponsored' terrorism – its *Patterns of Global Terrorism* has noted as one of the key trends 'a change from primarily politically motivated terrorism to terrorism that is more religiously or ideologically motivated'. Some of the most urgent concerns of security agencies now, such as the kind of suicidal commando-style attack launched by Lashkar e-Tayyiba in Mumbai in November 2008, have been overwhelmingly the work of religious groups.

In fact, the longest chapter in Bruce Hoffman's *Inside Terrorism*, an authoritiative recent study by the head of the Rand Corporation's terrorism research unit, is devoted to religion. Pointing out that none of the eleven identifiable terrorist groups that had been operating in 1968 could be classified as religious, Hoffman notes that the first 'modern' religious terrorist groups did not appear until around 1980. (He is using 'modern' here in the purely temporal sense.) By 1994, however, fully one-third (16 out of 49) of known terrorist groups 'could be classified as religious in character and/or motivation', and this proportion leapt again the following year to almost half (26 out of 56).

How far this reflects a change of perception as well as of reality is difficult to say; it is tempting to suggest that the phenomenon – or myth – of 'international terrorism', which was looking rather threadbare even before the collapse of the Soviet Union, found a replacement 'evil empire' as alarming, and maybe more plausibly international than the original. For it is undoubtedly Islam in particular rather than religion in general that engrosses Western attention: the fierce Binyamin Netanyahu, writing in the mid-1980s (ten years before he became a hawkish prime minister of Israel), typically focused only on 'Islam and Terrorism': 'in recent years few terrorists have matched the international prominence of those backed by the more extreme proponents of Islamic fundamentalism . . .'. A decade later, under the impact of a stream of attacks by Hezbollah, Hamas, Islamic Jihad, and others – many of them responses to the Jewish settlement programme fostered by Netanyahu himself – and culminating in the bombing of the World Trade Center in New York in 1994, that prominence had become overwhelming. The 11 September 2001 attack, of course, virtually blanked out all other terrorist activity: the pursuit of Osama bin Laden and al-Qaida became the 'war on terrorism'.

Religion and violence

Hoffman's terminology does raise some vital questions – not least the meaning of the description 'religious'. His definition, 'having aims and motivations reflecting a predominant religious character or influence', sounds like a Rand Corporation database criterion, and still leaves us wondering how we can measure the religious dimension of motivation. Hoffman gets closer to this when he goes on to propose the core characteristics of religious terrorism. First, it has a transcendental function rather than a political one: it is 'executed in direct response to some theological demand or imperative'. Second, unlike secular terrorists, religious terrorists often seek 'the elimination of broadly defined categories of enemies' and are undeterred by the politically counterproductive potential of indiscriminate killing. Finally, and crucially, they are not attempting to appeal to any other constituency than themselves.

This may indeed have terrifying implications: 'a sanctioning of almost limitless violence against a virtually open-ended category of targets'. But does it make sense to call this kind of violence terrorism? If we see terrorism as in some sense instrumental, it is hard to relate it to these motives. As Hoffman makes clear, its aim is elimination rather than persuasion (however indirect). The intended consequences of these acts simply cannot be delivered by anyone now alive. The object is, rather, a kind of cosmic revolution.

The fact that a number of writers, critical of the 'conventional wisdom' which holds that terrorism is a recent phenomenon, have invoked the long history of religious violence may also give us pause. The Muslim Cult of Assassins of the 12th and 13th centuries, like the Jewish Zealots of the firsst, have been enrolled for this genealogical purpose. But the suggestion that religious violence is analogous to modern terrorism throws into relief some serious issues. While the exact processes of modern terrorism may often be obscure, their core principle is the modern assumption that society can be changed by human agency. The practitioners of religious violence do not appear to be working on this assumption. The Assassins, for instance, although they were concerned with social change – the lapse of society from earlier standards of religious observance – were not concerned to convert people by direct action. Rather, they were testifying before God, a bilateral relationship which actually excluded the rest of the world.

A thoughtful comparative analysis of three religious groups, the Zealots, Assassins, and Thugs, by David Rapoport, indicates at least as many differences as similarities between them, particularly in the matter of intention. The Zealots may have aimed to provoke a general Jewish uprising against Roman rule, and thus have mixed (in Laqueur's phrase) 'messianic hope with political terrorism'. Getting at motives is difficult here, as so often, because the available commentaries – in this case

Josephus – are hostile or sceptical; but the marked element of messianism and the joyful embrace of martyrdom in the surviving accounts indicate a tangential relationship to politics. (Self-sacrifice can be a potent weapon in addressing a moral community, but is not necessarily related to earthly outcomes.) Likewise, the Assassins, whom one eminent Islamist describes as the first group to use 'political terror' in a 'planned systematic fashion', adopted a distinctly sacramental and suicidal method of killing governors, caliphs – and one Crusader king – with daggers in public on significant religious days. One study of political murder suggests that they 'contributed to the shaping of attitudes and behaviour no longer those of antiquity', but is cautious about what these were. Thagi (or Thuggee) – the cult of highway stranglers whom the British authorities in 19th-century India eventually suppressed – appears even further distanced from political action, in that its choice of victims was totally inscrutable to outsiders (and possibly the 'Thugs' themselves). Hinduism provides no scope for believing that society can be transformed, and hence for political action; at most the Thugs, in imagining themselves obligated to keep the world in balance, may be seen as defenders of the established order.

Destruction or persuasion?

Rapoport recognized that 'virtually all modern conceptions of terrorism assume that the perpetrators only mean to harm their victims incidentally'. This conception of indirect coercion is indeed vital to any view of terrorism as a rationally comprehensible instrumental process; but religious violence, as he shows, lacks this special dimension. It leaves the business of changing things up to God. In spite of all this, Rapoport remains concerned to maintain the analogy between premodern and modern terrorism, but to do so he has to characterize terrorism in a very elementary way. In fact, he writes of 'terror' and 'terror groups' rather than terrorism, and his key criterion is 'extranormality': the committing of 'atrocities, acts that go beyond the accepted norms and immunities that regulate violence'; 'extranormal or extramoral violence'; or more recently, 'violence which goes beyond accepted moral restraints'.

This emphasis on extranormality, as he notes, was (apparently firmly) established as a key element in the function of terror by the early analysts of terrorism, only to be reduced or removed by more recent writers. We may certainly accept that religious violence is exceptionally transgressive of social norms – particularly of modern expectations that violence will have some rationally comprehensible basis. So it may well be that religious violence can be characterized as 'terror'; but here it may perhaps be particularly important to maintain a distinction between terror and terrorism. However alarming religious violence may be, religious objectives – as explained by Hoffman and others – may lie outside the strategic scope of the concept, since they are beyond human agency. Even where an economic calculus is invoked, as in Osama bin Laden's assertion that 'more than $1 trillion losses resulted from these blessed attacks on 9/11', and that 'we are continuing this policy of bleeding America to the point of bankruptcy', the scale of the task must exceed any reasonable expectation. (But of course 'nothing is too great for Allah'.)

Is Netanyahu's remark that 'terrorism is uniquely pervasive in the Middle East, the part of the world in which Islam is dominant' an insinuation too far? It is also the part of the world that has produced more than one Jewish terrorist movement; while in the wake of the Oklahoma bombing – until 9/11 the most murderous 'terrorist' act of all time – we can hardly fail to see the destructive potential of Christian fundamentalism in the West itself. But it is not surprising that there has been an intense debate about whether Islam is a religion especially conducive to violent action. Samuel Huntington's idea that the upsurge of Islamist terrorism was a symptom of a 'clash of civilizations' met with a chorus of official disapproval, but it certainly mirrored the jihadis' own view. Their ultimate aim is a total transformation of the world.

Religion into politics

It is possible that the very idea of fixing boundaries between religious and ethnic motivation is problematic, since these boundaries are highly permeable. How, for instance, should we measure the religious symbolism evident in EOKA graffiti in Cyprus, or in the gable-end paintings of 'mass rocks' in republican Belfast? Indeed, the very notion of isolating the 'religious' element in the motivation of a group, to establish whether or not it is 'predominant', is rooted in Western political culture, with its sharp division between church and state, sacred and secular. It may have limited value even in the West, where the syndrome of sacral or 'holy nationalism' has been far more pervasive than most people have recognized. It can only be applied to other cultures with extreme caution. In the case of 'primitive' animist religions, the impossibility of circumscribing the spiritual sphere is well understood, maybe because peoples such as the Nuer of the Sudan have always been studied by anthropologists – nowadays a very sophisticated bunch. Islam, on the other hand, which has been the province of Western experts called 'Orientalists', 'Arabists', or 'Islamists', with a rather heterodox disciplinary background, has tended to bamboozle Western analysts. It has been argued that the relative neglect of Islamic studies stems from the fact that Islam does not conform to expectations raised by the idea that it followed in the footsteps of other 'religions of the book'. Expecting it to follow a progressive sequence from Judaism and Christianity, Westerners failed to grasp the strength of the ancient Arab cultural bedrock within the structure of belief capped by the intransigent monotheism of Muhammad; God as the ultimate controlling agency is superimposed on an animist infrastructure. Studies of mainstream religious culture in Egypt and elsewhere are demonstrating a world where the natural and supernatural are inextricably interlaced.

The key point is that Islam is a religious culture which resists the separation of secular from spiritual jurisdiction – Bernard Lewis says 'the very notion of a secular authority is seen as an impiety'. And though others suggest that in the later 20th century the standardizing pressure of state power has steadily eroded this traditional resistance, it is noticeable that over the last decade 'fundamentalist' critiques of 'bad Muslim' states – notably by the *Salafiyya* – have markedly intensified. The question whether such opposition should take a violent form is a complex one. The concept generally invoked in discussions of terrorism, that of *jihad*, is often presented as an inbuilt incitement to violence. But the standard translation, 'holy war', may be misleading (the tag 'holy' is certainly a Western addition for the reasons we have just seen), since *jihad* literally means 'striving', and might better be rendered as 'struggle'. Some modern Muslims hold that it refers to spiritual struggle, or at most to defensive rather than aggressive war, but fundamentalist jihadis certainly do not accept this. But if it is, as they maintain, a religious obligation to maintain a state of war with those outside the community of Islam, can terrorism properly understood fulfil this function?

Messianism and millenarianism

Are there reasons why acts of extreme, norm-transgressing violence, 'atrocities' as Rapoport calls them, should be generated by religious conviction? Two appear particularly significant. The first is what is often called 'fanaticism', the capacity of religious belief to inspire commitment, and its resistance to compromise. The second is messianism, the expectation of imminent transformation of the world. Both of these have their secular parallels (or shadows); revolutionaries of all sorts have routinely been labelled fanatics (as indeed have baseball or football club supporters), and some of them at least have shown plain indications of millenarian hope that dramatic action could wreak a sudden realization or acceleration of prophecy.

A third element, which may not justify violence itself but which valorizes its use, is the belief that death in a sacred cause is the proper end of life. This too has its secular echo in such ideas as (what Wilfred Owen called 'the old lie') *dulce et decorum est pro patria mori*, but in some religious belief systems it is taken much further. Much of Islam's negative image in the West is surely due to its apparent propensity to encourage sacrificial or suicidal action by *mujahideen*, holy warriors – including children. Under the alarming headline 'British Muslims take path to jihad: Kashmir terror group claims suicide bomber was from Birmingham', for instance, a British newspaper assembled all the elements of this image, reporting that the founder of the London-based Islamic group al-Muhajiroun claimed to have sent some 1,800 young men to 'military service' overseas. Recruited at mosques and university campuses across the country, they went to fight against infidel 'occupying forces' in Kashmir, Palestine, and Chechnya. 'People who sacrifice themselves to Almighty God as human bombs will achieve martyrdom and they will go to paradise', the 'Syrian-born cleric' is quoted as saying.

The open embrace of death amplifies the culture shock inherent in the fact that the leaders of these groups – most notoriously the council, *Majlis al-Shoura*, of Hezbollah in Lebanon – are Anglicized as 'clerics', or even 'clergymen'. Indeed, Western reporting of Hezbollah (the Party of God) most dramatically represents the heady, even disorienting impact of the fusion of Islam and terrorism. Originating in the enthusiasm generated by the Iranian revolution of 1979, Hezbollah has always mixed strident fundamentalist calls with firmly grounded local political action. It became a significant force with the Israeli invasion of Lebanon in 1982, which has provided its actual, as distinct from rhetorical, targets, and generated its substantial public support. Many of its operations, especially in its early phase – the bombing of the US embassy in Beirut in April 1983 and the colossal truck-bombing of the US Marine and French forces headquarters that October (killing over 300 troops) – and its later hostage-taking period, may fit the label 'terrorist', which is universally applied to the organization. Even these actions,

13. Self-sacrificial determination on public display: Hezbollah fighters commemorate a martyred comrade in Beirut, May 1996

however, have a recognizable military dimension. Many others have been highly discriminate guerrilla attacks on the military positions of the Israeli army (IDF) and its ally the South Lebanon Army. (And nothing so indiscriminate as the Sabra-Chatila massacres, the IDF's shelling of Beirut, or indeed the US Navy's bombardment of September 1983.)

In this confrontation, which can only be described as a territorial liberation struggle (the word 'national' is even more problematic in Lebanon than anywhere else), Hezbollah has become increasingly effective in a military sense: in the last five years of the 20th century, its casualty ratio relative to the IDF improved from more than 5:1 to less than 2:1. Its rhetoric remains unchanged: calling for not only the total destruction of Israel, but also a larger life-and-death struggle against 'the West' (of which Israel is merely the agent). The violence of this struggle is aimed at exterminating rather than intimidating the enemy; in this sense it may not sensibly be called terrorism. These blood-curdling demands no doubt merit the media attention they get in the West, but some analysts point to a more pragmatic dimension. Acting as a 'paramilitary militia' it has steadily crushed the formerly dominant Amal grouping and established itself as a genuinely political organization – which recognizes, for instance, the impossibility of its orginal commitment to establishing Lebanon as an Islamic state.

Suicide and self-sacrifice

'Suicide bombings' – or 'martyrdom operations' – undoubtedly get under Western skin with a special acuteness. A century ago Mahatma Gandhi observed how Western humanism's ever more strident insistence on the supreme value of life had distanced it from other religious traditions, and indeed its own Christian roots. He saw suicide action as subversive, precisely because it could not be instrumental. To defeat England it was necessary not to kill Englishmen but 'to kill ourselves'. The declaration by the 7/7 bomber Shehzad Tanweer that 'we love death the way you love life' was profoundly shocking to many, including those who denounced the bombers as members of a 'death cult'.

Suicide attacks have multiplied dramatically – there have been three times as many since 2000 as in the previous twenty years – and some have produced visible strategic results. For instance, the hugely destructive suicidal attacks on American and French installations in Lebanon contributed to the withdrawal of those countries' forces from Lebanon, with significant medium-term political effects. But thinking about this issue is fraught with difficulty, not least because in the nature of things there is often no conclusive evidence whether the incidents were simply high-risk operations rather than deliberate sacrifices. Even the 9/11 hijackers may not all have been told of the finality of their mission. In some attempted car and truck bomb attacks in Lebanon in the 1980s, it appears that the drivers did not know that thay had been chosen to become martyrs by remote control.

However, the Hamas campaign launched in the summer of 2001, when a truck loaded with explosives drove into an Israeli army checkpoint in Gaza, produced a series of genuine and disturbing examples. The claim of Sheikh Ahmed Yassin, the founder and leader of Hamas, that 'all the Palestinians are ready to become martyrs', may be an exaggeration, but seems to be more than merely rhetorical. Amongst the most destructive (politically and psychologically) of all Middle Eastern terrorist attacks were carried out by the 'quiet young men' who walked into Ben Yehuda Street, crowded with similiarly young Jews at the end of the sabbath, and detonated shrapnel bombs strapped around their waists. The astonishing footage shot by Hamas of Nafeth Enether blowing himself up in an attempt to kill Jewish settlers in the Gaza Strip provided the most vivid evidence of this commitment.

The line between readiness to die and suicide is, ultimately, a very fine one. Suicide is normally, in time of peace, forbidden for

Muslims just as it is for Christians (such as IRA hunger-strikers). But in war, as with the Armenian Christian celebration of 'death knowingly embraced', it may confirm the fidelity of the patriot or the believer. And undoubtedly the motives of individuals may differ from those of organizations; 'movements that sponsor suicide bombings are not themselves suicidal'.

Fundamentalism

Are these religious or political motives? For all their messianic semitones, Hezbollah and Amal are very real political forces engaged in an earthly power struggle, as indeed is Hamas in Palestine. The dense fusion of territorial, ethnic, and sectarian impulses in the Lebanese civil war clearly operate in other 'fundamentalist' challenges to modernizing secular governments, in Algeria and Egypt as well as Iran and Afghanistan. The underlying ideology of these movements, Islamism, emerged half a century ago; only in the last decade, however, has the West begun to grasp how it differs from old-style fundamentalism. This timelag is a product in part of stereotyping (as Edward Said would argue, the rooted Western 'orientalist' blindness to nuance and change in the Muslim world). Deep cultural differences of this kind cannot be understood without some considerable effort, and this effort has seldom been forthcoming. This general indifference has been jolted by 9/11, and the question will be how long the new spirit of inquiry will last.

Islamism has been a significant movement in Egypt since the establishment of the Muslim Brotherhood by a schoolteacher (just for once, not a 'cleric'), Hasan al-Banna, in 1928. Banna's aim was to counteract the subversion of Islamic values through the Westernized education system, and he was one of the first to posit in stark terms an opposition between Islam and 'the West' as total, incompatible value systems. In Egypt, which was subject to a protracted and demoralizing domination by Britain (the 'veiled protectorate'), the tension was acutely felt. The Brotherhood flourished, with 500 branches established by 1940, and 5,000 by 1946 – each maintaining a mosque, a school, and a club. By that time, a small inner organization of 'spiritual messengers' was also engaging in sporadic terrorist attacks, aimed first at killing traitors to Islam.

In the later 1940s, the government took aggressive steps to crush the Brotherhood, banning it in 1948 and assassinating al-Banna in 1949. The establishment of an independent republic under Gamal Abdel Nasser (whom the Brotherhood tried to assassinate in 1954) brought more comprehensive repressive measures, culminating in 1965 with the full-scale suppression of the organization, and the arrest and execution of al-Banna's most influential successor Sayyid Qutb. But Qutb's martyrdom only confirmed the force of his argument that Islam was under merciless assault by Westernization, and must be defended by physical as well as spiritual methods.

The pervasive strength of Islamism was indicated by the decision of Nasser's successor Anwar Sadat – who made political capital of his Muslim identity – to lift the ban on the Brotherhood. In 1981, Sadat himself was assassinated in the most spectacular manner, while taking the salute during a big military parade. This action was clearly in part a reaction to Sadat's historic accommodation with Israel, and to recent mass arrests of religious 'extremists' (both Muslim and Coptic Christian), but it also signalled an intensifying assault on the viability of the secular Egyptian state by two formidable offspring of the Muslim Brotherhood, the Islamic Group (*Gamat al-Islamiya*) and al-Jihad. Al-Jihad completed the logic of the Islamist argument by insisting on the centrality of 'the forgotten obligation', armed struggle: 'There is no doubt that the idols of this world can only be removed by the power of the sword.' This did not yet mean terrorism: al-Jihad planned the Sadat assassination as a *coup d'état*, a trigger for a mass rebellion – which never materialized. The organization suffered ferocious repression by the regime of Hosni Mubarak in the following years. But recruitment to such groups tends to be stimulated rather than strangled by repression, and in this case these losses were more than made good by the return of hundreds of volunteers who had gone to Afghanistan to fight with the Taliban *mujahideen* against the Marxist government. (Ironically, of course, these were the fighters who were funded by their greatest enemies, the USA.)

> There is only one place on earth which can be called the house of Islam, and it is that place where an Islamic state is established and the Sharia is the authority and God's laws are observed . . . The rest of the world is the house of war.
>
> God has established only one cause for killing – when there is no other recourse – and that is *jihad*. He has defined the aim of the believer and the aim of the disbeliever in the most clear and decisive manner:
>
> 'Those who believe fight for the sake of God. And those who disbelieve fight for the sake of idols. Fight, then, the followers of Satan; surely the guild of Satan is but feeble.'
>
> Sayyid Qutb, *This Religion of Islam* (1967)

These holy warriors, frequently labelled fundamentalists, represent a direct engagement with the modern world rather than a simple repudiation. One historian of Islam suggests that although the Islamist message draws on 'premodern' readings of the Koran and other religious texts, it 'is wholly modern in its revolutionary existentialism' – the first Islamist group to emerge in Egypt after Sayyid Qutb's execution was inspired not just by Islamic writings but by the 'propaganda of the deed' advocated by ultra-leftist radicals such as the Baader-Meinhof gang. In the late 1980s, these groups shifted to a wholly terrorist campaign, aimed at the tourist industry – a target that was particularly shocking in the West (which was only slowly beginning to grasp that tourism might not always be wholly 'innocent'), and that combined assault on the West itself with economic subversion of the Egyptian state. A series of shootings at tourist buses and Nile cruises in late 1992 was followed by large-scale machine-gun and hand-grenade attacks of such visible targets as the Europe Hotel in Cairo in 1996, and the massacre of 58 tourists at the temple at Luxor in 1997. The economic damage was significant – approaching 2 billion US dollars in lost revenue at the turn of the century. So although the ultimate mechanism invoked by these groups is God – the Islamic Group announced in 1996 that it would 'pursue its battle' faithfully 'until such time as God would grant victory' – there is also a materially measurable scale of effectiveness in play. And it is clear that where they have sufficient military strength, as in Afghanistan, Islamist movements do not limit their use of violence to a demonstrative or symbolic dialogue with God, but carry the ideal of *jihad* into the sphere of open warfare.

The struggle in Afghanistan after the Soviet intervention in 1979 formed a conduit for the emergence of perhaps the most problematic of all terrorist movements, al-Qaida. Originating simply as a contact group for the Arab volunteers who joined the Afghan resistance, al-Qaida eventually served as a framework to extend the inspirational leadership of Osama bin Laden across the world as its members left Afghanistan after the withdrawal and collapse of the USSR in 1989. Its structure remained a mystery – certainly to the US intelligence services – at least until the 9/11 attacks. It was bound by a core idea rather than a formal organization, and its method of defending Islam was transformed by the events of the Gulf War in 1991. Until his offer to raise a military force to defend Saudi Arabia against the threat of Iraqi invasion was rebuffed by the Saudi government, bin Laden seems to have envisaged conventional military action as paramount. The Saudi acceptance of US intervention dramatically magnified, for bin Laden, the Western danger long predicted by al-Banna and Qutb. The 'crusaders' had returned, and had to be resisted by any possible means: the kinds of action could range from the bombing of US embassies, through the almost-successful bombing of the World Trade Center in New York in 1994, to the attack on the USS *Cole* in Aden harbour on 12 October 2000.

The ascending destructiveness of these actions may be a product of luck as much as of strategy, though they surely signalled that bin Laden's declaration of war on the USA in August 1996 was more than a rhetorical gesture. After the New York bomb in particular, which might have caused stupendous destruction but for a minor error of placement, the fact that the September 2001 attack came as an almost total surprise indicates how easy it remained to underestimate both the perseverence and the technical sophistication of Islamist groups. Yet Ramzi Yousef, the bomb's designer, had projected the collapse of both towers. He clearly announced that his object was to make America realize that it was 'at war' by suffering casualties on the scale of Hiroshima and Nagasaki: 'this is the way you invented . . . the only language in which someone can deal with you.'

The terms of the 1996 declaration – 'the Jihad on the Americans occupying the Country of the Two Sacred Places' – were directly related to US foreign policy (it included an historical account of US policy since Franklin D. Roosevelt's time, as well as detailing the corruption and un-Islamic policies of the Saudi state). But there is more at stake for the jihadis than particular American policies. The USA – the 'Great Satan' – takes its place in a grand narrative of Muslim victimhood in which the West's consistent efforts to dominate and destroy Islam have led to the humiliating political fragmentation and social impoverishment of the Arab-Muslim world. The only solution is the establishment of a truly Islamic state in which the disjunction between religion and politics would be terminated. This might seem to require a miraculous transformation of the world, but it is clear that the jihadis can find an actual model for such a 'miracle' in the early expansion of Islam under Muhammad himself.

Notwithstanding its historicizing rhetoric, al-Qaida powerfully fuses Islamist ideology with exploitation of modern technology to demonstrate that modernization does not (as most modernizers since Ataturk have assumed) require 'Westernization'; it can be turned against the West in the struggle to restore true Islam. Western analysts have gradually come to see that it is not permanent organizations but transient 'networks' that are now likely to generate Islamist attacks. Factors like locality and friendship, rather than religious faith, are at the core, or 'hub', of these networks. The Internet as much as religious institutions provides their medium. What impels the attackers is the desire to avenge perceived injustices against Muslims anywhere in the world. As Mohammed Sidique Khan, one of the London bombers of 2005, declared, 'I am directly responsible for protecting and avenging my Muslim brothers and sisters'. The only real strategic debate amongst jihadis seems to be over whether priority should be accorded to targeting the 'far enemy' – the USA and Western Europe – or the 'near enemy' – the pseudo-Muslim regimes such as those in Egypt or Saudi Arabia.

Finally, we need to recall that 'fundamentalism' is not the exclusive preserve of Islam. Consider, for instance, the Jewish group Gush Emunim, which, with dizzying recklessness of the political consequences, planned in 1984 to destroy the sacred enclosure of the Haram ash-Sharif in Jerusalem. In doing this, they gave real life to a fear had impelled Arab resistance to Zionism from the start, but which Zionists had always laboured to dismiss as a Muslim fantasy. Kahane stands normal political logic on its head: 'it is our refusal to deal with the Arabs according to halakhic obligation that will bring down on our heads terrible sufferings'. (In other words, the thing to be feared is not the enmity of the Arabs, or even the whole world, but the displeasure of God.) As Rapoport notes, fundamentalist Jews stress the genocidal violence of the original Jewish conquest of Israel – when God accompanied them in person – and maintain that the

14. 191 people were killed and nearly 2,000 wounded when 10 bombs exploded on 4 commuter trains in Madrid between 7.37 and 7.40 a.m. on 11 March 2004. The bombers were an *ad hoc* 'leaderless' Islamist group, coming together through the social network rather than formal organization

exterminatory concept of *herem* remains not merely justified but obligatory to preserve the Jewish state.

The aim of extermination rather than intimidation may seem to stretch the concept of terrorism too far. Activism might be a more accurate, but too tame, a term here, while genocide in this context describes an aspiration rather than an action. But the ultimate objective – securing the land – remains firmly political. We are presented with a political logic that is alien and perhaps incomprehensible to the Western tradition, but can be seen to be very different from the apparently total detachment from political logic manifested by the most purely 'religious' activist groups.

In this perspective, the most completely 'religious' activists are those of the fringe cults which, like the Aum Shinrikyo and the other (by one count) 183,000 in Japan alone, rest on millenarian visions that cannot conceivably be realized by any human agency. (Even assuming they can be grasped in the first place.) These cults are perhaps not uniquely a product of advanced technological communities, but their proliferation in the *fin-de-siècle* period seems to owe something to frustration with the complacent materialism of 'the end of ideology'. As with the small-group terrorism of the 1970s, they touch a raw nerve in societies that are sometimes conscious of overdevelopment, and mildly neurotic about the possible abuse of high technology. The Aum's release of sarin gas on the Tokyo underground on 20 March 1995 opened a genuinely terrifying prospect of mass murder (subsequent police raids found enough sarin in Aum's possession to kill over 4 million people). With such violence we reach what may be seen either as the purest, or the most absurd, reduction of terrorism to symbolic gesture.

Chapter 7
Countering terrorism

> Miss Blum always said she didn't belive in security
> anyway. 'Least of all from *those* people, they come when
> they feel like it, out of a clear blue sky in the middle
> of the night.'
>
> Heinrich Böll, *The Safety Net* (1979)

So what is to be done about terrorism? Are there better and worse
ways of responding to it? Certainly there is a multiplicity of
possible responses, ranging from mild regulation to full-blooded
military repression. What are the possible benefits, and what are
the likely costs? Is it possible that sometimes the cure may be worse
than the disease? In particular, as Laqueur asked, 'can a
democratic society subdue terrorism without surrendering the
values central to the system?'

Antiterrorist, counterterrorist?

Probably the biggest hazard inherent in reactions to terrorism is
the impulse towards imitation. For many years, it was common to
draw a clear distinction between 'antiterrorist' measures and
'counterterrorism'. The former described every lawful step a state
might take, from special legislation to martial law; the latter meant
the adoption of terrorist methods – such as assassination and
indiscriminate reprisals – by the state's own forces. This distinction

is still sometimes maintained, but more often it has been eroded. Whether this signals an adjustment of the concepts themselves is not clear; as elsewhere, the main outcome seems to be another blurring of definition. 'Counterterrorism' now clearly predominates; Wikipedia is an exception in preferring the traditional form. The Patriot Act set up, amongst other things, a 'counterterrorism fund'. Although some writers on terrorism do draw a distinction, they do not agree on what the terms signify (one says that 'in contrast to counterterrorist measures, antiterrorist steps are largely defensive in nature'; others hold that 'counter terrorism is a passive response', while antiterrorism 'is an aggressive and potent tool of government'). Usually, though, the two terms are now used interchangeably, without any explicit or implied distinction. Most worryingly, perhaps, the British government also uses both terms in its legislation. But in spite of this apparent unconcern, we need to keep in focus the sorts of issues about the degeneration of liberal-democratic norms implicit in phrases like 'resort to' or 'descent into counterterrorism'; for a variety of reasons, states can all too easily go too far.

Threats and responses

In thinking about appropriate ways of reacting to terror, it remains important to keep in mind the distinction between war-related terror and terrorism as an independent strategy. On a dispassionate assessment of the actual threat posed by 'pure' terrorism, the most appropriate reaction might well be to ignore it altogether. In statistical terms, it is a far less substantial danger than road traffic accidents, and very much less amenable to preventive action. And even after 9/11, it is not evident that it fits the American mantra of 'clear and present danger' – a criterion specifically designed to inhibit the tendency of governments to exaggerate threats. There is no visible terrorist force ready to strike. Does this mean that, as Tony Blair said, the old 'rules of the game' are no longer sustainable in face of a new kind of threat?

For democracies, action against terrorism is not at all simple. The responses available to some kinds of regimes are not part of the democratic repertoire. Walter Laqueur cites the example of Iran after 1979, where the government 'killed without discrimination, extracted information by torture, refused to extend medical help to injured terrorists. And it broke the back of the terrorist movement.' Whether or not this is a true case of cause and effect, it is clearly not an option for the 'liberal state', whose remedies have to be more careful, time-consuming, burdensome, and expensive. Heinrich Böll's *The Safety Net* (*Fursorgliche Belagerung*), written at the height of the left-wing terrorist campaign in West Germany, sets us inside the elaborate kind of security system that could follow – Miss Blum's scepticism notwithstanding – and raises sharp questions about its larger implications.

It has been argued, for instance by Robert Goodin, that the best public response to terrorism is simply 'fearlessness'. Just going to work or using public transport after an attack such as 7/7 is the most effective thing ordinary people can do. Richard English has pointed out that amidst the public alarms in the wake of 9/11 people lost sight of their own experience of terrorism – they had learned to live with it for many years. But politicians have shown little inclination to preach equanimity: rather the reverse. The UK Defence Minister went as far as to declare in October 2010 that 'the world is more dangerous than at any time in recent memory'. He was not asked to justify this proposition. In political terms, the option of ignoring terrorism, however rational, is unprofitable. Terrorism operates precisely by playing on the deep-seated public need for, and anxiety about, security of life and property. As a threat to the survival of the state, terrorism is implausible if not absurd but as a challenge to the state's monopoly of force and the broader sense of public security, it is acutely effective. It is no coincidence that it has flourished most spectacularly in a modern Western world which since the 19th century has achieved an unprecedented level of public security, together with dependence on an extremely complex infrastructure. The pressure of public anxiety is inevitably greatest in democratic societies, where various public representatives, including a free and professionally alarmist media, will certainly demand action even if ordinary people do not. But being seen to 'do something' is not easy when the opponent is invisible. Governments soon develop, as Adam Roberts says, 'a powerful thirst for intelligence' which can quickly lead to bending or breaking legal constraints in the search for information. It can lead to increased police powers, detention without trial, far-reaching changes in legal procedures, and the use of torture, or its milder relation 'inhuman and degrading treatment'.

Proportionality and aptness

What, if any, limits should be set to action against terrorism? The BBC journalist David Jessel, making a *Heart of the Matter* report in 1985, noted that even 'keeping a sense of proportion in the face of terrorist atrocity may seem a counsel of appeasement. What moral constraint, after all, binds the terrorist?' If there are to be limits, they will reflect the underlying ethos of the society that is under threat or attack. For those societies that think of themselves as the bearers of 'Western civilization', Jessel suggested that the principle of proportionality, as prescribed by St Thomas Aquinas, 'stands up remarkably well to a modern view of justice and expediency'. The reaction of a state should be in proportion to the wound inflicted on it; such action should not merely add to the volume of violence; and the outcome of any counterattack should not lead to a greater injustice than that which was the original provocation.

In the case of conventional war, proportionality is (at least in theory) calculable. Even there, though, mistakes have often been made. Even conventional military forces are difficult to measure exactly, and the enemy's political intentions are all too easy to misread. Clausewitz made the apparently simple point that 'the first of all strategic questions and the most comprehensive' is for decision-makers to be clear about what a situation *is* and what it *is not*. Any illusion of simplicity here dissolves when terrorism is at issue, since we are driven back to the fundamental problem of defining the nature of terrorism and the threat it represents. It is *not* an invasion; can it in any real sense be subjected to military action?

The clarity demanded by Clausewitz is very hard to achieve. It is rare, for instance, to find a member of the Rand Corporation such as Jeffrey Simon, writing (unofficially) in 1987, urging the need to stand back and ask fundamental questions – such as whether vital US interests were 'really threatened by international terrorism'. Simon noted that 'for years Washington has allowed the natural emotional abhorrence of terrorism to supplant a rational evaluation of the terrorist danger'. The debate over military responses to terrorism was 'fuelled by the American public's and government's growing frustration and anger toward the new enemy', and the possibility that 'there may be no solution to this one' – or only solutions lying beyond US control, had simply not been considered.

Yet, as he warned, the continuing expectation that terrorism can be beaten raised the stakes in the conflict and placed American foreign policy at further risk. The problem was that each terrorist attack turned into 'an assault on national pride and honour'. The distinction between national honour and national security became blurred. Persistent evidence of the tendency of military reactions to terrorism to further a cycle of violence was ignored, as was the fact that 'terrorists can reverse any counterterrorist "victories" with one well-placed bomb'. Simon urged that the USA should tone down the national reaction, and accept terrorism as a fact of life rather than diverting valuable resources to an endless conflict.

That, of course, was long before the destruction of the Twin Towers in New York. The assertion that 9/11 had 'changed everything' swept all before it, and swept aside such arguments as these. It offered perhaps the ultimate test of the military response. The USA, on behalf of civilization, declared war not just on existing terrorist organizations but on terrorism itself. Never – even in July 1914 – had the appropriateness of military action been more confidently asserted. The dizzying reach of this commitment was confirmed in President Bush's Thanksgiving address to the 101st Division two months later:

> America has a message for the nations of the world. If you harbour terrorists, you are terrorists . . . And you will be held accountable. We will not be secure as a nation until all of these threats are defeated. Across the world, and across the years, we will fight these evil ones.

To some degree no doubt this rhetoric was a necessary palliative for a traumatized nation, but coming amidst a fierce and – in terms of international law – illegal assault on the Taliban regime in Afghanistan, it had sobering implications. And within six months, the USA launched a still more far-reaching assault on the regime of Saddam Hussein in Iraq, which had no apparent connection with al-Qaida.

The 'global war on terror' was launched under the justification of self-defence, which to many people seemed to be self-evidently invoked by the attack. The advocates of military action were not required to demonstrate that 9/11 was the opening of a new kind of conflict, rather than an old-style terrorist act on a larger scale. The idea that terrorist organizations could be located and destroyed in the manner of conventional targets was hardly subjected to any public dispute at the outset. (Rare objections came from the distinguished military historian Sir Michael Howard, who urged more painstaking, less cathartic methods, and the former Monty Python star Terry Jones, who first raised the question whether it was possible to make war on an abstract noun.) The USA had already established a firm pattern of armed reaction: most recently illustrated in President Clinton's 'Operation Infinite Reach' of August 1998 in retaliation for the truck-bombing of US embassies in Nairobi and Daar-es-Salaam in which 259 people (12 of them Americans) were killed. Cruise missiles were launched at targets in Afghanistan stated to be training camps run by Osama bin Laden, and a chemical warfare plant in Sudan. 'Our target was terror', Clinton announced. Yet here as elsewhere, the choice of targets was disputable; the strike on the Al Chifa plant in Khartoum, in particular, may have been an error.

Even without such intelligence mistakes, or 'collateral damage', the distinction between retaliation, reprisal, and mere revenge is not easy to maintain when an enemy cannot be identified or located with exactness; and the utility of indirect retaliation has always been doubtful. Adam Roberts has highlighted the long tradition of scepticism about punitive raids as reprisal for terrorism, noting that since attacks on leaders 'proved spectacularly wrong in Tsarist Russia . . . it would be deeply ironic if it were to be reincarnated in the name of counterterrorism'. The invasion of Iraq in 2003 turned into perhaps the most spectacularly deadly of all such strategic mistakes. By the time President Bush admitted that there was 'no evidence that Iraq was involved in the September 11 attacks', the coalition was fighting a protracted internal war in which over 100,000 Iraqi civilians would die. It was hard to see either proportionality or aptness in this, since most experts saw the war as a breeding ground of new, more loose-knit terrorist groups. A decade after 9/11, many agencies still seemingly believed that terrorist networks could be taken down by removal of their 'masterminds', and that smart weapons and pilotless drones could achieve this without counterproductive political effects.

Strategic choices

The spectrum of policy choice starts, perhaps, from the option of reading terrorism as a symptom of social injustice and responding by reform. In some cases, such as ethnic separatist movements, straightforward concessions may in principle remove the cause of violence. The 'root causes' (a phrase mocked by neoconservatives since 9/11) of other social problems are less straightforward, and their relation to terrorist action less direct. But in all cases, the option of political adaptation is open to the potent objection that it is a concession to – and so an encouragement of – violence. As a rule, therefore, reform is offered (if at all) as a reward for an explicit abandonment of violence, a confession of error, and a demonstrative embrace of democratic principles. The balance here between which should come first can be so fine – as it was for many years in Northern Ireland – that the political ('peace') process is effectively paralysed. If so, in the meantime antiterrorist action will be taken to hold the ring, to limit violence to what a British minister once unguardedly called 'an acceptable level'. Where reform is not on offer, or terrorism is read as criminality, there may be a more determined effort to extirpate it, involving systematic offensive measures, and even what may be described as 'retaliation' against communities held to be sheltering terrorists. Where terrorism is read as a manifestation of madness or evil, that effort may be full-blooded.

Whatever the overall political intention, antiterrorist action needs to be more discriminating and calibrated than terrorist action. To help in charting the range of responses available, whether for anti- or counterterrorist policy, we may draw a basic distinction between passive and active measures. On the whole, passive measures are shaped by the nature of terrorist acts – airport security is a response to hijacking and sabotage of aircraft, defensive steps labelled 'target hardening' a response to bomb attacks, the 'safety net' of individual security measures a response to kidnapping, and so on. They are an effort to shrink the windows of opportunity available to terrorists. They are also a tacit admission of the impossibility of predicting terrorist action. Active measures may try to address this by engagement with terrorist groups with the aim of capturing or destroying them. The only chance of sucess in this direction lies in an effective intelligence system, using techniques such as infiltration and surveillance to acquire accurate information. Modern states typically possess large and expensive intelligence services, but their record of success in providing this kind of information is patchy at best. The 9/11 attacks happened in a country which spent huge sums on agencies like the FBI and CIA, yet failed to establish effective countermeasures, despite the warning delivered by the bomb attack on the World Trade Center in 1994, and the definite identification of Osama bin Laden's organization as a major threat to national security (bin Laden was on the FBI Ten Most Wanted list for years). Typically, as it emerged, a July 2001 report by an FBI agent in Arizona highlighting the number of Middle Eastern men taking flying lessons and a keen interest in airport security was simply shelved by his superiors.

When carefully developed intelligence is coupled with ruthlessness in action, as in postwar Israel, the result may be the accurate targeting of leaders of terrorist organizations. Yet even after this has been done repeatedly, it has not succeeded in significantly reducing the level of terrorist attacks. Its achievement is usually more speculative – it has contained or prevented other terrorist actions that would have occurred. As with all intelligence operations, exact evaluation of such claims is not possible. Nor indeed is it possible to dispute the larger promise advanced by successive Israeli prime ministers that retaliation will not merely contain but defeat terrorism. The fieriest sermon on this text is still Netanyahu's book *Terrorism: How the West Can Win* (1986), whose conflation of terrorism and terrorist groups was eventually echoed in the 2001 'war against terrorism' proclaimed by President Bush – and amplified with alacrity by Ariel Sharon in Israel.

15. Attacking the 'infrastructure of terrorism' in Gaza: an Israeli military incursion at Beit Hanoun, 15 December 2001

The government of Israel maintained that its military assaults on West Bank towns like Bethlehem, Nablus, and Jenin (under the seductive title 'Operation Protective Shield') would indeed curb the danger of suicide attacks on its people. Its people largely agreed; few disputed the notion of targeting 'the infrastructure of terrorism' – though Uri Avneri (co-founder of the peace group Gush Shalom) denounced it as nonsensical – 'the "terror infrastructure" exists in the souls of millions of Palestinians...' – and the view of an IDF soldier that 'I'm pretty sure that all the suicide bombers inside Israel have blown themselves up, and the ones still in the territories are either being killed or being caught' was followed the next day by yet another suicide bombing in Haifa.

The most spectacular act of retaliation, the assassination of Osama bin Laden by US special forces in the Punjab garrison town of Abbottabad on 1 May 2011– after nearly ten years of the most expensive manhunt in history – raised all these questions. The long delay in finding him drew as much comment as the manner of his death. Though the US at first claimed he had been killed resisting arrest, it became clear that he was unarmed. If this was 'justice', as President Obama asserted, it was far removed from due process. Bin Laden was killed not because he could not be captured, but because (as with the Guantanamo detainees) it was impossible to convict him in court. This told its own story, as did the decision to consign his corpse to the seabed – criticised as impermissible by some leading Islamic authorities – to prevent his grave becoming a 'terrorist shrine'. Was the world 'a safer place' as a result, as Barack Obama also declared? This was debatable. Bearing in mind bin Laden's already circumscribed activity, and the potential hostile public reaction to the breach of Pakistani sovereignty, this may be another case when (as Jeffrey Simon noted) national security took second place to national honour.

Domestic policy

A further key distinction should be made between policies that are under the control of individual states, and those which depend on (often problematic) international cooperation. The former have a much higher chance of being put into effect, but that effect may be limited: they may literally run out of road at the state's borders. Policies available to states fall into three categories: laws, forces, and operational methods.

States in general, even – perhaps especially – democracies, have little difficulty in establishing the basic elements of antiterrorist action. Although governments are nowadays more likely to come under public pressure to 'do something' rather than to take a minimalist line, they have a fair bit of freedom in deciding whether to adopt an essentially legal approach or to step outside the law. While it is rare to go direct to action like Israel's policy of assassinating those it identifies as terrorists, the option of modifying the law is a tempting one. Special emergency laws, for instance, which may restrict or abrogate civil liberties in order to provide the security forces with greater powers of surveillance, search, or detention of suspects, have often been rapidly enacted in the wake of terrorist attacks, without much parliamentary or public opposition.

Special powers may or may not need special forces to implement them. Terrorist campaigns that specifically target the police or the political section of the police (like the IRA versus the G Division of the DMP (Dublin Metropolitan Police) in 1919) may shake their morale sufficiently to impel states either to fall back on military forces – with possibly disagreeable political implications – or to set up what is sometimes called a 'third force'. But the creation of special security forces is quite a hazardous policy, for democracies at least. Great Britain, for example, has never established a third force within the UK, though it came very close with the 'Black and Tans' in Ireland in 1920–1 (a force with arguably did more than anything else to undermine the British effort to keep Ireland within the UK). This bruising experience, followed by a still more dubious initiative in Palestine with the establishment of 'Special Night Squads' under the leadership of Orde Wingate to pre-empt the actions of Arab 'terrorist' groups during the rebellion of 1936–9, and again – briefly and embarrassingly – against Zionist terrorists after 1945, may have persuaded Britain that the dangers outweigh the advantages. Germany has been cautious in keeping its specialist antiterrorist force GSG9 as part of the panoply of civil policing – albeit the distinct 'border guard police' (*Grenzschützgruppen*). Israel, on the other hand, has established special military forces (which have acquired an unenviable reputation for ruthless pre-emptive or punitive action with a high risk of 'collateral damage' to innocent people who, either through chance or through military intelligence mistakes, have found themselves in the wrong place at the wrong time).

Whether these forces have contained or provoked terrorist action is a contentious issue. The recent case of the Abbayat clan in Bethlehem, which, after the death of two successive leaders in Israeli missile assassinations, actually tightened its organizational grip on the town, instead of splintering as the Israelis seem to have expected, is one of many which may give pause. (The third generation of leaders were besieged in the Church of the Nativity during the Israeli military incursion in April and May 2002, and deported under the international arrangement which ended the siege.) The criteria of success can, indeed, be drawn up in significantly different ways. For instance, the action of the US Delta Force in seizing an Egyptian airliner on Italian soil after the *Achille Lauro* hijacking in 1985 has been portrayed as a success, although it might well have triggered a serious international incident by violating Italian sovereignty. The more insidious danger of such forces, however, is likely to arise when they are deployed for an extended period in a quasi-police role. In a situation of protracted domestic conflict such as Northern Ireland, the capacity of a semi-clandestine force like the SAS – though this is in strict terms a military and not a 'third' force – to set the policy agenda is likely to increase. Such forces will inevitably stray beyond strict legality from time to time, and if this becomes a persistent tendency it will eventually subvert the key principles of liberal society: above all, perhaps, 'due process'.

Still, if there are hazards to the use of special forces, there are problems in mounting certain kinds of antiterrorist operations without them. The problems are produced by the inherent ambiguity of the terrorist strategy, and the fact that it usually operates in a complex political environment. In the grey zone between politics and warfare which terrorism inhabits, it is always likely that actions will lie outside the experience and repertoire of either the police or the army, and will need civil–military coordination of a kind that has never been easy to achieve. The precise timing and technique, for instance, of a wide range of operations from searches and arrests to the storming of buildings or hijacked aircraft, is likely to be critical, and the political implications of mistakes may be far-reaching. The degree of training needed is not likely to be achieved on an ad hoc basis, as is only too obvious from the chequered (but generally depressing) history of airline security, a low-prestige service, dangerously underfunded, especially in the USA, and especially in comparison with the exotic intelligence agencies. As one commentator has pointed out, an unsettling aspect of the 9/11 attacks was that the hijackers did not 'slip past' some incompetent individuals: they passed through checkpoints in four different airports and no inspector noticed what they were carrying.

The international difficulty

It has always been clear that antiterrorist action needed to be international as well as domestic if it were to be effective. (Conrad's *Secret Agent*, Verloc, was employed on just such a design, on the part of an illiberal central European state, to lever Britain into an antiterrorist coalition). More recently, one of the more prolific writers on terrorism held that it was 'the failure of the international community to fully recognize terrorism as criminal behaviour' that had 'encouraged the growth of terrorist activity over the last two decades'. But the whole problem – as acute in 1937 as during Tony Blair's visit to Syria in October 2001 – was that no usable common definition of terrorism, least of all 'as criminal behaviour', could be reached. After the assassination of King Alexander of Yugoslavia, the League of Nations Council adopted a resolution (10 December 1934) that 'it is the duty of every state neither to encourage nor tolerate on its territory any terrorist activity with a political purpose'; states should do all in their power to prevent and repress terrorist acts, and to assist other states to do so. For the next three years, a League committee laboured to draft international conventions for the prevention and punishment of terrorism. It defined 'acts of terrorism' (carefully avoiding the generic term 'terrorism' in the hope of skirting the thorny issue of political motivation) as 'directed to the overthrow of a government or an interruption in the working of public services or a disturbance in international relations, by the use of violence or by the creation of a state of terror'.

The convention's deployment of neutral terminology, however, failed: individual states (notably Great Britain) still resisted committing themselves to its possible implications. The British Home Office found the committee's three terrorist objectives rather ill-sorted – 'between two appalling catastrophes is sandwiched an interruption of public services, which many people would consider to be of a much lower order of magnitude, and in many cases quite well justified'. Here as ever was the rub: one man's legitimate protest was another's revolutionary crime. 'The crux of the position', the Home Office said, 'is that the Convention would place us under an international obligation to punish sympathisers here who encourage or help oppressed minorities abroad to secure political liberty, if other than purely peaceable methods (which would probably be useless) are employed.'

Since the 1930s, international cooperation has advanced by quite small stages, always limited by the absence of consensus on the justifications for political violence. In October 1970, the UN General Assembly resolved that it was the duty of states 'to refrain from organizing, instigating, assisting or participating in acts of

We know that terrorism is an international problem that requires the concerted efforts of all free nations. Just as there is collaboration among those who engage in terrorism, so there must be cooperation among those who are its actual and potential targets. An essential component of our strategy, therefore, is greater cooperation among the democratic nations and all others who share our hopes for the future. We have achieved some successes. But too often countries are inhibited by fear of losing commercial opportunities or fear of provoking the bully. The time has come for nations that truly seek an end to terrorism to join together, in whatever forums, to take the necessary steps.

US Secretary of State George Shultz, 1986

civil strife or terrorist acts', but subsequent committees established
to define terrorism and recommend methods of preventing it failed
to do either. Debate has persistently been diverted towards
political analyses – of underlying causes, and of the claims of
various groups to be excluded from the terrorist category. From
one perspective, this shows that 'the General assembly has
clearly elevated the right to self-determination above human
life'; from another, it reflects the belief that freedom is worth
dying for. Whatever else may have changed after 9/11, this
tension did not – as was made clear by President Assad of Syria
when Tony Blair tried to enlist him for the international
coalition against terrorism in October 2001: 'We differentiate
between resistance and terrorism. Resisistance is a social,
religious and legal right that is safeguarded by UN
resolutions ... Can anyone accuse de Gaulle of being a terrorist?'
Assad added a general caveat against the idea of a war on terror:
'Terrorism works as a network. It does not have a certain head,
either as a person or in terms of an organization.' This unpalatable
analysis may, however, have been too mystical for Westerners to
absorb.

The most successful international measures have focused on
particular offences, like attacks on 'internationally protected
persons' – primarily diplomats – and hostage-taking; and on
the protection of nuclear material and the prevention of
transfer of terrorist finances. But larger frameworks have remained
hard to construct, and key organizations like Interpol (which is
barred by its constitution from investigating political matters)
remain limited in their capacity. The ideal mechanism for
international action would be a single global statute. But
in 2001, only six European states had specific antiterrorist laws,
and these were quite varied in their terms. In the absence of a
single legal framework, the viability of international action
devolves to a great extent on the process of extradition – on the
principle *aut dedere aut judicare* – and this remains fraught
with complications.

Though there have been significant regional steps, in particular the 1977 European Convention for the Suppression of Terrorism, the process of ratifying this agreement has been erratic (Ireland did not adopt it until 1986, for instance); and it still baulked at the basic task of defining a terrorist offence. There are grounds for qualified optimism in the case of Ireland, whose judges (notably in the case of Dominic McGlinchy, whose appeal against extradition to Northern Ireland on a murder indictment was turned down in 1982) paved the way for adoption by substantially narrowing the previously capacious view of 'political offences'. So although some recent British extradition requests have failed, these have been on technical, 'strict construction' grounds – wrongly drawn up affidavits. At the same time, the French refusal to extradite Abu Daoud, wanted in both Germany and Israel for his part in the Munich massacre, to either country in 1977 stands as a warning of the capriciousness of *raison d'état*.

State sponsorship

The US State Department specifies four key elements of US counterterrorism policy:

> First, make no concessions to terrorists and strike no deals;
> Second, bring terrorists to justice for their crimes; Third, isolate
> and apply pressure to states that sponsor terrorism to force them
> to change their behavior; and Fourth, bolster the counterterrorism
> capabilities of those countries that work with the US and
> require assistance.

The high profile of state-sponsored terrorism in the official US analysis has always been striking. As against this, though, it is rare to find any attempt to provide precise assessment either of its contribution to the total volume of terrorist activity, or of the role of sanctuaries in the growth of terrorist organizations. Before 1989, it was common to see such broad-brush estimates as, for instance,

16. Al-Qaida fighters captured in Afghanistan, transported to Guantanamo Bay, Cuba, facing an uncertain future as suspected 'illegal combatants'

that '80 per cent of terrorist groups in the world are at least superficially Marxist . . . and claim the right to support from the Soviet Union'. The sudden and unexpected disappearance of the Evil Empire seems to have impelled the State Department to allow (in 2001) that 'state sponsorship has decreased over the last several decades', but again nothing like a quantitative estimate has been offered. Later in the decade, it maintained that state support 'compounds' the threat of terrorist organizations, and even that it was 'critical' – though it immediately diluted this with the less stringent suggestion that without state sponsorship terrorist groups would have 'greater difficulty' in securing funds, weapons, and so on.

A world in which 80% of terrorists were not Marxists but Muslims might present a totally different kind of issue. But the American response to 9/11 showed that little had changed, except the roster of 'usual suspects': Afghanistan, Iraq, and Sudan in place of the rogue states of the 1980s Libya, Syria, and Iran. (Though George W. Bush soon rescued the last of these, and added North Korea for good measure, when he identified his 'axis of evil'.) The theory of state sponsorship may be weakly developed but its practical significance is immense: it validates the direct retaliation which has become an established American policy preference. A belief in the deterrent effect of 'smart' munitions (quicker and simpler than intelligence work, certainly) has survived a surprising amount of contrary evidence. Most vitally, it allows the superpower to act unilaterally, untrammelled by the differing policy approaches and concerns of partners (witness, for instance, its brusque – even brutal – treatment of Italy in the aftermath of the *Achille Lauro* hijacking). Even when the USA was, rhetorically at least, most committed to building an international 'coalition against terrorism', in the wake of the 9/11 attacks, it was clearly not prepared to accept any modification of its own agenda.

Whether in a perfectly controlled, rogue state-free world, terrorism would actually be eliminated may not have been the point in all this. There was at least room for suspicion that the threat of terrorism was being used as a pretext for striking down disagreeable regimes. The central problem that remained unaddressed was the survival potential of ideological/religious movements like al-Qaida, which combine a potent cause with a flexible, one-size-fits-all organization. The ability of its members like Mohammed Atta, the hijacker of American Airlines flight 11, to operate for long periods in Germany and even the USA itself, indicates that traditional notions of sanctuary may be even less relevant than they were in the past. State sponsors may be a luxury rather than a necessity for such protean movements.

Cost and effectiveness

If we look for precise evaluation of the effectiveness of antiterrorist policies we find it is surprisingly thin on the ground. Very few indeed of the many writers on terrorism have produced a statistical analysis of key countermeasures. Particularly surprising (in the light of Adam Roberts's plausible suggestion that in democratic states 'the principles of any counterterrorist campaign are likely to be articulated extensively and scrutinised closely') is the fact that none of the many official reviews of the British antiterrorist legislation carried out over the last 40 years has adduced any concrete evidence on its effectiveness – or apparently seen the need to do so. One such review, by Lord Colville in 1987, noted that during his enquiries he had heard 'the serious suggestion' that 'if all emergency legislation were abolished, the situation would at least be no worse'. Legally, this may be true; psychologically, it may not. Although other jurists have also declared that the ordinary law would be as effective as the special legislation, British governments have sidestepped the issue.

Twenty years ago Grant Wardlaw posited as an elementary step 'the development of a comprehensive classification' of security functions which could inform decision-makers and avoid confusion. There is still little evidence that this basic step has been taken, so that while it is easy enough to compile lists of possible antiterrorist measures, together with their fiscal and, so to speak, civil-libertarian costs, there is nothing like a ready-reckoner to evaluate their comparative effectiveness. For instance – a policy-maker might well want to know what, precisely, is the value of identity cards in countering terrorism? They can only guess. And are the objections 'emotional rather than rational', as one expert says? How can the long-term costs be computed? On the sensitive issue of computerized intelligence information, the British expert Richard Clutterbuck offers only that 'for the time being this, like many other civil liberties, must depend ultimately on trust, on the integrity of those with access to power over the liberty of others'. This is less reassuring than he seems to think.

Democracy against terrorism

There can be no dispute that terrorism is 'undemocratic' in that it ignores all conventional processes of representative politics. But does it go further than this? Is it inherently antidemocratic? And are democracies uniquely vulnerable to terrorism? We have already noted that democratic states may be more sensitive to the threat that terrorism is seen to present to public safety. It is a commonplace to see terrorism as an attack on democratic principles; one prolific terrorism expert has even specified that 'the democratic process is a key target' for terrorists, though he does not explain exactly how. (It is surely rare for elections and parliaments to be directly attacked.) He seems to be referring to the contempt of both left- and right-wing extremists for liberal democracy – and the probability that if they came to power they would replace it – but this is not quite the same thing.

A study by the Dutch political scientist Alex Schmid identified four key weak points of democracies in face of terrorism: (i) freedom of movement, (ii) freedom of association, (iii) abundance of targets, and (iv) the constraints of the legal system. On this model, the vital features of democratic societies are openness, tolerance, legality, and a high valuation of human life. These features also generate countervailing strengths – free elections and freedom of speech reduce 'the need for political violence to bring about social change', or simply to make a case in public, and judicial procedure protects the rights both of individuals and of minority groups. But Schmid seems to see these strengths as limited to minimizing the likelihood of terrorist action, rather than as means of coping with a terrorist campaign once begun. Like many analysts, he seems to be less impressed by the potential resilience of democratic societies under terrorist attack than by their impotence. It is rare to find a suggestion such as Jeffrey Simon's that 'equating the threat terrorism poses to individuals with its challenge to Western democratic societies underestimates the ability of Western societies to withstand periodic terrorist campaigns'.

Others have noted that while terrorism's impact on the legitimacy of governments, and on the delicate trust that exists within a democracy can be considerable, the threat to democracy posed by terrorist acts is less important than the response that such acts evoke. This view has been recently amplified by a political scientist who holds that democratic societies are particularly 'vulnerable to a form of violence that incites governments to overreact' and so lose legitimacy; she suggests that the primary danger to legitimacy and stability lies in failure to preserve key values of the democratic order such as individual rights, the rule of law, and limited government. This is in a sense merely to reformulate the basic problem, but Kimbra Krueger makes another important point: that the principle of proportionality – the most effective means of maintaining legitimacy – is difficult to act on because of the tendency of democratic states to be hung up on 'the peace/war dichotomy'. Terrorism is categorized either as crime or as warfare; democratic institutions are not designed or equipped to deal with the grey area that terrorism occupies. While this may present an acutely difficult dilemma for 'new democracies', it may also pose long-term problems for older structures.

One of the central mainstays of democratic culture, not included in Schmid's list, but a matter of acute concern for many others, is freedom of the press and other media. Even the cautious Grant Wardlaw says that media reporting of terrorist incidents 'has very damaging effects', but like most writers has difficulty specifying what these are. It is less often registered that the main contribution of the media is to 'the perception more than the reality of the terrorist threat', as Simon notes, and that it tends to widen and dramatize the public notion of the threat. More commonly and intemperately, analysts and politicians have asserted that publicity is the 'oxygen' of terrorism. In 1981, Yonah Alexander, referring to the enigmatic Symbionese Liberation Army, held that 'for several years, the media have continued to magnify the case out of proportion to its real significance', and in so doing had actually transformed it into an internationally known movement possessing power and posing an insurmountable problem to the authorities. More generally, he held that terrorists make 'a conscious and deliberate effort to manipulate the media' and that 'by providing extensive coverage of incidents the media give the impression that they sympathise with the terrorist cause'.

The 'oxygen of publicity' argument implies that control of the media might offer a way of choking off terror altogether. But as British experience with the 'broadcasting ban' shows, this is not easy to achieve in a deeply-rooted liberal culture. Alexander notes that attempts to impose media blackouts are likely to drive terrorists to escalate their violence, and that 'an unjustifiable limitation of free media will ultimately result in the victory of terrorism'; he advocates self-restraint and voluntary cooperation with the criminal justice system, but also says that 'the determination of a proper role for the media should not be left to their judgement alone'. Whose, then? This is the difficulty.

Freedom or security?

One reason why accounts such as Schmid's stress – to the point perhaps of exaggeration – the weakness of democratic societies, is that they focus not on the expression of public will (in Isaiah Berlin's famous distinction, 'positive freedom') but on the guarantees of individual liberty ('negative freedom') which are so characteristic of Western liberalism: freedom of movement, assembly, speech; protection against arbitrary government; equality before the law – in Anglo-Saxon terms 'due process'.

Within the composite of liberal democracy, it seems to be liberalism rather than democracy that is the perceived source of vulnerability to internal violence. The crucial assumptions of the civic culture: toleration, moderation, reasonableness, non-violence, form the conditions for the exercise of 'civil liberties'. Terrorism, however defined, is certainly a calculated assault on the culture of reasonableness.

It is also, surely, liberalism rather than democracy that is threatened, not so much by violence itself as by the state's reactions to it – often, as Schmid notes, propelled by popular demands. While he recognizes that 'the recourse to unlawful methods of repression' will ultimately undermine the government's legitimacy, he does not address the possibility that antiterrorist measures may fundamentally corrode or subvert the constitutions which they aim to defend. It is here that the problem of defining terrorism and evaluating the threat it poses becomes acute; the very imprecision of the concept and its operation leads to loose definition of the powers taken to oppose it, while (as in war) the blanket of national security smothers the interrogative powers on which public accountability depends. Without the effective interrogation of legislation and executive action there is no liberal democracy.

The vital issue is the point at which the liberal legal system becomes unable to cope with organized violence. This issue was identified with rare clarity in Lord Gardiner's judicial review of Britain's antiterrorist measures in 1975:

> when normal conditions give way to grave disorder and lawlessness, with extensive terrorism causing widespread loss of life and limb... the courts cannot be expected to maintain peace and order in the community if they have to act alone. The very safeguards of the law then become the means by which it may be circumvented.

Lack of information, and the intimidation of witnesses and jurors, can paralyse the legal system. The response may be to create special courts, special laws, and special forces, all of which may over time represent a shift towards a 'strong state' or even a 'garrison state'. Such a course has in the past been assumed to be deeply alien to British traditions, but it may be that during the 20th century there has been some movement in this direction.

We need to keep in mind that special laws, the further they depart from ordinary law, carry corrosive possibilities for even a robust and long-established liberal tradition; the risk of 'normalizing the extraordinary', and eroding hard-won safeguards – especially in the absence of any open procedures for assessing that the measures are proportionate to the danger. Just how far terrorism could threaten the survival of liberal-democratic principles became clear with Britain's 1988 'broadcasting ban', preventing the voices of Sinn Féin leaders from being heard. This was justified by two arguments: the apprently technical, though unproven, assertion that terrorists lived on 'the oxygen of publicity'; and the wholly illiberal assertion that the right of the victims of terrorism to be shielded from the sound of terrorists' voices should outweigh the right of other citizens to information. This particular experiment was widely mocked, and eventually undermined by a combination of its evident ineffectiveness and the need to bring the banned leaders back into the political 'peace process'; but it remains a disturbing illustration of the fragility of even entrenched liberal assumptions.

Since 9/11 the level of threat to 'due process' has risen along with the amplification of public alarm. The US Patriot Act (a laborious acronym of 'Providing Appropriate Tools Required to Intercept and Obstruct Terrorism') removed many legal restrictions on internal surveillance. The USA's treatment of the 'illegal combatants' held at Guantanamo has been profoundly disturbing to many Americans and many more in the world at large. The torture of terrorist suspects has even been publicly advocated by an American law professor – a proposition scarcely imaginable in the West in modern times. Not, of course, that torture has not been used by modern Western states, but there has been a prevailing belief that (quite apart from moral objections) the intelligence it secures is inherently unreliable. Certainly, Western jurisprudence rests on the inadmissibility of evidence so extracted. Even less spectacular departures from the conventions of due process, such as the British device of 'control orders' for terrorist suspects who could not be convicted in open court, may have had the effect, as Lord Macdonald put it in January 2011, of making British institutions a 'symbol of hypocrisy' to the outside world.

So far, the question whether civil liberties are compatible with antiterrorist action remains unanswered. Ronald Crelinsten's thoughtful analysis ends with an extremely demanding agenda: 'security intelligence agencies must watch out for threats ... within the context of the value our democratic societies place on individual rights'. At the heart of the issue remains the problem of information: most of the special antiterrorist powers, such as detention or deportation of suspects, depend on precise, accurate information if they are not to be abused. Can such accuracy be assured without constructing a surveillance system so comprehensive as to represent a danger to individual rights in itself? It has been cogently argued that secret intelligence collection poses fewer problems for civil liberies than has traditionally been claimed, but only on the assumption that governments can establish a public consensus, overcoming what one intelligence analyst calls the pervasive 'lack of clarity over the nature of the threat which society faces, the purposes for which intelligence is being collected, and the uses to which it is being put'.

This would seem to require an open and probably complicated public debate. Something like this did indeed begin to happen in Britain, despite the persistent efforts of the Labour government to smother public criticism of its antiterrorist legislation after 9/11.

In July 2010, Lord Macdonald was given 'independent oversight' of a major official review of British antiterrorism measures, which itself indicated a new climate of caution about the consequences of over-reaction. Its terms of reference were to 'look at the issue of security and civil liberties, and where possible to provide a correction in favour of liberty'. Macdonald himself publicly declared that Britain had 'over-reacted' after 9/11, and that 'we saw some powers, some laws which did go too far'. Though some of the most-criticized (and possibly effective) elements of 'control orders', for instance, were removed, their replacement by 'Terrorism Prevention Investigation Measures' struck many observers as mainly cosmetic. And in the end, no major public debate was triggered by the review.

The USA provided a demonstration that public consensus can itself overwhelm definition and debate: while a handful of

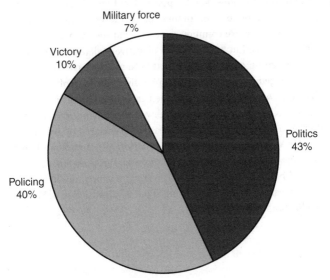

17. **How 268 terrorist groups worldwide ended, 1968–2006**

academic lawyers might warn that 'the rights of terrorist suspects are our rights too', mainstream American opinion appeared contemptuous of such liberal scruples. The Patriot Act had broad public approval. As Crelinsten soberly remarks, 'Most people will sacrifice their freedom for security if they feel threatened enough.'

How terrorism ends

It is unlikely that terrorism as such will ever end. But most individual terrorist campaigns so far have indeed come to an end, and the way they have ended is instructive. A Rand corporation analysis of 648 terrorist groups operating between 1968 and 2006 found that ten percent had achieved 'victory'; while a slightly smaller proportion had been crushed by direct military force. The two biggest reasons for termination were police investigation (40%) and some kind of political settlement (43%). Around 62% of all terrorist groups had disappeared, but only 32% of religious groups had done so. None of them had achieved 'victory'. Recently, it has become more common to accept that the 'global war on terror' launched in 2001 with the objective of defeating 'every terrorist group of global reach' was both misconceived and mismanaged. (Indeed, the British Foreign Secretary officially declared the concept wrong-headed early in 2009.) This rather belated realization is in itself somewhat depressing, and the fact that – to judge by the official threat levels declared by Britain and the USA – the whole decade of counterterrorist action has had no measurable effect, might be even more so. But these histories should help to sustain belief that terrorism is no more likely now than it was a century ago to bring about the destruction of Western civilization.

References

Chapter 1

definitions: Martha Crenshaw, 'Current Research on Terrorism: the Academic Perspective', *Studies in Conflict and Terrorism* 15 (1992); Sunil Khilnani, 'The Politics of Terrorism', *Political Quarterly* 64, 3 (1993)

fear: C. A. J. Coady, 'The Morality of Terrorism', *Philosophy* 60 (1985); Robert E. Goodin, *What's Wrong with Terrorism?* (London: Polity Press, 2006)

agitation/enforcement: T. P. Thornton, 'Terror as a Weapon of Political Agitation', in Harry Eckstein (ed.), *Internal War: Problems and Approaches* (New York: Free Press of Glencoe, 1964)

strategies: Martha Crenshaw, *Revolutionary Terrorism. The FLN in Algeria 1954–1962* (Stanford: Hoover Institute Press, 1978)

pity and remorse: Edgar O'Ballance, *The Language of Violence: The Blood Politics of Terrorism* (San Rafael, CA: Presidio Press, 1979)

women: Luisella Neuburger and Tizana Valentini, *Women and Terrorism* (London: St Martins Press, 1996); Geula Cohen, *Woman of Violence. Memoirs of a Young Terrorist* (New York: Holt, Rinehart, and Winston, 1966)

Chapter 2

international convention: League of Nations First Conference on the Repression of Terrorism, Geneva, 1937. Public Record Office, London, HO 45 1801

international terrorism: Brian Jenkins, 'International Terrorism: the Other World War', in Charles Kegley (ed.), *International Terrorism: Characteristics, Causes, Controls* (New York: St Martins Press, 1990); Kent L. Oots, *A Political Organization Approach to Transnational Terrorism* (New York: Greenwood Press, 1986); Thomas C. Schelling, 'What Purposes Can "International Terrorism" Serve?', in R. G. Frey and C. W. Morris (eds.), *Violence, Terrorism, and Justice* (Cambridge: Cambridge University Press, 1991)

state sponsorship: Yonah Alexander, 'State Sponsored Terrorism', Centre for Contemporary Studies (Occasional Paper No. 3), London, 1986

superterror: Ehud Sprinzak, 'The Great Superterrorism Scare', *Foreign Policy* No. 112 (Fall 1998); Jessica Stern, *The Ultimate Terrorists* (Cambridge, MA: Harvard University Press, 1999); Thomas Copeland, 'Is the "New Terrorism" Really New?', *Journal of Conflict Studies* (Winter 2001); Graham Allison, *Nuclear Terrorism* (New York: Times, 2004)

Chapter 3

French Revolution: 'Commission temporaire de Commune-affranchie', quoted in Richard Cobb, *Terreur et Subsistences* (Paris: Librairie Clavreuil, 1965); Colin Lucas, 'Revolutionary Violence, the People and the Terror', in Keith M. Baker (ed.), *The Terror* (Oxford: Oxford University Press, 1994)

Georges Sorel: M. Anderson, 'Georges Sorel, Reflections on Violence', *Terrorism and Political Violence* 1, 1 (1989)

fascism: A. J. Gregor, 'Fascism´s Philosophy of Violence and the Concept of Terror', in David Rapoport and Yonah Alexander (eds.), *The Morality of Terrorism* (Oxford: Oxford University Press, 1982)

Nazism: Jeremy Noakes, 'The Origins, Structure and Function of Nazi Terror', in N. O´Sullivan (ed.), *Terrorism, Ideology and Revolution* (Brighton: Wheatsheaf Books, 1986)

Latin America: Amnesty International, Final Report of the Mission to Chile, April 1974; Robert Cox, 'Total Terrorism: Argentina, 1969 to 1979', in Martha Crenshaw (ed.), *Terrorism, Legitimacy and Power* (Middletown, CT: Wesleyan University Press, 1983)

ultras: Martha Crenshaw, 'The Effectiveness of Terrorism in the Algerian War', in Martha Crenshaw (ed.), *Terrorism in Context* (University Park, PA: Pennsylvania State University Press,

1995); Michael Barkun, 'Millenarian Aspects of "White Supremacist" Movements', *Terrorism* 1, 4 (1989)

Chapter 4

concepts: Martha Crenshaw, 'The Concept of Revolutionary Terrorism', *Conflict Resolution* XVI, 3 (1972); Ariel Merari, 'Terrorism as a Strategy of Insurgency', *Terrorism and Political Violence* 5, 4 (1993)

anarchists: Ulrich Linse, ' "Propaganda by Deed" and "Direct Action"; Two Concepts of Anarchist Violence', in W. Mommsen and G. Hirschfeld (eds.), *Social Protest, Violence and Terror in Nineteenth and Twentieth Century Europe* (London: Macmillan, 1982); Peter Kropotkin, *Le Révolté* (Geneva, 1880), quoted in W. Laqueur, *The Terrorism Reader* (London: Wildwood House, 1979)

FALN: Carlos Marighela, *For the Liberation of Brazil* (Harmondsworth: Penguin, 1971)

Tupamaros: Maria Esther Gilio, *The Tupamaros* (London: Secker and Warburg, 1972)

urban guerrillas: Martin Oppenheimer, *Urban Guerrilla* (Harmondsworth: Penguin, 1970); Anthony Burton, *Urban Terrorism: Theory, Practice and Response* (London: L. Cooper, 1975)

groupuscules: Bommi Baumann, *Terror or Love? The Personal Account of a West German Urban Guerrilla* (London: John Calder, 1979); R. Drake, 'Contemporary Terrorism and the Intellectuals: The Case of Italy', and B. Cordes, 'Euroterrorists Talk About Themselves: A Look at the Literature', in P. Wilkinson (ed.), *Contemporary Research on Terrorism* (Aberdeen: Aberdeen University Press, 1987)

Chapter 5

Armenians: Khachig Tololyan, 'Cultural Narrative and the Motivation of the Terrorist', *Journal of Strategic Studies* 10, 4 (1987); Michael Gunter, 'Contemporary Armenian Terrorism', *Terrorism* 8, 3 (1986)

Irish republicanism: Charles Townshend, introduction to P. J. P. Tynan, *The Irish National Invincibles and their Times* (first published 1894; reprinted Millwood, NY: Kraus Reprint, 1983); M. Taylor and E. Quayle, *Terrorist Lives* (London: Brassey's, 1994)

Basques: R. Clark, 'Patterns of ETA Violence: 1968–1980', in P. Merkl (ed.), *Political Violence and Terror* (Berkeley: University of California Press, 1986); W. Douglass and J. Zulaika, 'On the Interpretation of Terrorist Violence: ETA and the Basque Political Process', *Comparative Studies in Society and History* 32, 2 (1990)

Chapter 6

definitions: Bruce Hoffman, *Inside Terrorism* (London: Victor Gollancz, 1998); David Rapoport, 'Fear and Trembling: Terrorism in Three Religious Traditions', *American Political Science Review* (1984)

messianism: David Rapoport, 'Why Does Religious Messianism Produce Terror?', in P. Wilkinson (ed.), *Contemporary Research on Terrorism* (Aberdeen: Aberdeen University Press, 1987)

Islam: Mark Anspach, 'Violence Against Violence: Islam in Historical Context', *Terrorism and Political Violence* 3, 3 (1991)

Hezbollah and Hamas: A. R. Norton, 'Hizballah: From Radicalism to Pragmatism', *Middle East Policy* 5, 4 (1998); Matthew Levitt, *Hamas: Politics, Charity and Terrorism in the Service of Jihad* (New Haven and London: Yale University Press, 2006)

suicide: Ariel Merari, 'The Readiness to Kill and Die: Suicidal Terrorism in the Middle East', in W. Reich (ed.), *Origins of Terrorism: Psychologies, Ideologies, Theologies, States of Mind* (Cambridge: Cambridge University Press, 1990); Abdelwahab El-Affendi, 'The Terror of Belief and the Belief in Terror: On Violently Serving God and Nation', in M. Al-Rasheed and M. Shterin (eds), *Dying for Faith* (London: Tauris, 2009)

fundamentalism: Al-Jihad, quoted in John L. Esposito, *The Islamic Threat: Myth or Reality?* (New York: Oxford University Press, 1992), p. 135; Malise Ruthven, 'Signposts on the Road', *Times Literary Supplement*, 7 December 2001; *A Fury for God* (London: Granta Books, 2002)

9/11: Don DeLillo, 'In the Ruins of the Future', *Harper's Magazine*, December 2001

near and far enemies: Mary Habeck, *Knowing the Enemy: Jihadist Ideology and the War on Terror* (New Haven and London: Yale University Press, 2006)

Chapter 7

measuring threats: Walter Laqueur, 'Reflections on Terrorism', *Foreign Affairs* (Fall 1986)

proportionality: Jeffrey D. Simon, 'Misunderstanding Terrorism', *Foreign Policy* 67 (1987); Adam Roberts, 'Terrorism and International Order', in L. Freedman et al. (eds.), *Terrorism and International Order* (London: Routledge and Kegan Paul, 1986)

international action: Home Office minute, 20 July 1937, Public Record Office, London, HO 45 18080; Martha Crenshaw, *Terrorism and International Cooperation* (New York: Westview Press, 1989)

state sponsorship: US Department of State, 'Overview of State-Sponsored Terrorism', *Patterns of Global Terrorism*, http://www.state.gov/www/global/terrorism/2001/report/sponsor.html

democracy: Alex P. Schmid, 'Terrorism and Democracy', in A. Schmid and R. Crelinsten (eds.), *Western Responses to Terrorism* (London: Frank Cass, 1993); Kimbra L. Thompson Kruger, 'The Destabilisation of Republican Regimes: The Effects of Terrorism on Democratic Societies', *Low Intensity Conflict and Law Enforcement* 5, 2 (1996)

media: Alex P. Schmid, 'Terrorism and the Media: The Ethics of Publicity', *Terrorism and Political Violence* 1, 4 (1989)

extralegal measures: Alan Dershowitz, *Why Terrorism Works* (New Haven and London: Yale University Press, 2002), Chapter 4

conclusion: Ronald D. Crelinsten, 'Terrorism, Counter-Terrorism and Democracy: The Assessment of National Security Threats', *Terrorism and Political Violence* 1, 2 (1989); Seth G. Jones and Martin C. Libicki, 'How Terrorist Groups End', RAND Corporation Research Brief, 2008

Further reading

General

Two books by Walter Laqueur, *Terrorism* (London: Little, Brown, 1977) and *The Terrorism Reader* (London: Wildwood House, 1979) provide a concise historical background; his more recent *The New Terrorism: Fanaticism and the Arms of Mass Destruction* (Oxford: Oxford University Press, 1999) is more prolix and more alarmist, with an extensive bibliographical essay – whose only major lacuna is, oddly, the topic of 'fanaticism', so loudly announced in the book's title but sketchily treated in the text. Grant Wardlaw, *Political Terrorism: Theory, Tactics and Countermeasures* (Cambridge: Cambridge University Press, 1982, 1990) is a judicious analysis, while Bruce Hoffman, *Inside Terrorism* (London: Victor Gollancz, 1998) is a useful survey from the Rand Corporation perspective, hard-nosed and unsentimental. For a more radical perspective, see Richard Falk, *Revolutionaries and Functionaries: The Dual Face of Terrorism* (New York: Dutton, 1988). Louise Richardson, *What Terrorists Want: Understanding the Terrorist Threat* (London: John Murray, 2006), and Richard English, *Terrorism: How to Respond* (Oxford University Press, 2009) thoughtfully analyse historical experience. In the spate of books following 9/11, one or two are still worth reading, such as Strobe Talbott and Nayan Chanda (eds.), *The Age of Terror* (New York: Basic Books, 2001). Cindy C. Combs, *Terrorism in the Twenty-First Century* (Upper Saddle River, NJ: Prentice Hall, 1997) is a college textbook that reveals much conventional wisdom on the subject.

State terror

Most writing on terror is workmanlike rather than brilliant, but an important exception is Eugene V. Walter's essay in historical anthropology, *Terror and Resistance* (New York: Oxford University Press, 1969). Most conservative writers avoid the subject of state terror (the extensive section headed 'state terrorism' in Laqueur's *New Terrorism*, for instance, proves to be all about 'state-sponsored' terror – a completely different subject – on the part of the USSR, Libya, Iran, and Iraq), so much of the commentary comes from a radical perspective: a fair example is William D. Perdue, *Terrorism and the State* (New York: Praeger, 1989). Alexander George (ed.), *Western State Terrorism* (Cambridge: Cambridge University Press, 1991) contains several challenging essays, including a fierce critique of 'The Discipline of Terrorology' by the editor, who notes that his prime subject, Paul Wilkinson, 'unlike many in this area, is not a raving madman'. There is a comparative study of two Latin American cases in David Pion-Berlin, *The Ideology of State Terror: Economic Doctrine and Political Repression in Argentina and Peru* (Boulder, CO: L. Rienner, 1989).

Revolutionary terror

The classic study of Russian populism is Franco Venturi, *Roots of Revolution* (New York: Knopf, 1960). Zeev Ivianski, *Individual Terror: Theory and Practice* (Tel Aviv: ha-Kibbutz ha-Meuchad, 1977) is a lucid analysis. The contribution of women to revolutionary violence in Tsarist Russia is evoked in Vera Broido, *Apostles into Terrorists* (New York: Viking Press, 1977). For the anarchists in general, see George Woodcock, *Anarchism* (Harmondsworth: Penguin, 1962), and in particular Martin A. Miller, *Kropotkin* (Chicago: Chicago University Press, 1976). Martha Crenshaw's study of the FLN in Algeria, *Revolutionary Terrorism* (Stanford: Hoover Institute Press, 1978) is an exemplary fusion of particular analysis with a wide theoretical vision. More idiosyncratic, but interesting, is Richard E. Rubinstein, *Alchemists of Revolution: Terrorism in the Modern World* (New York: Basic Books, 1987). A densely written but rewarding analysis of small-group terrorists in Italy and Germany can be found in Donatella della Porta, *Social Movements, Political Violence and the State* (Cambridge: Cambridge University Press, 1995).

Nationalist terror

On the IRA, M. L. R. Smith, *Fighting for Ireland? The Military Strategy of the Irish Republican Movement* (London: Routledge, 1995) presents a level-headed academic examination; Patrick Bishop and Eamon Mallie, *The Provisional IRA* (London: Heineman, 1987) and Peter Taylor, *Provos: The IRA and Sinn Fein* (London: Bloomsbury, 1997) are excellent journalists' investigations.

ETA is, unsurprisingly, less well covered in English, but see John Sullivan, *ETA and Basque Nationalism* (London: Routledge, 1988) and Joseba Zulaika, *Basque Violence* (Reno, NV: University of Nevada, 1988).

The logic and methods of Zionist groups are illuminated in Yehuda Bauer, *From Diplomacy to Resistance* (New York: Atheneum, 1973); on the Lehi, see Joseph Heller, *The Stern Gang: Ideology, Politics and Terror 1940-1949* (London: Frank Cass, 1995); on the Irgun, Menachem Begin's memoir *The Revolt* (London: W. H. Allen, 1979) is obligatory reading, while there is an absorbing account of their most famous operation in Thurston Clarke, *By Blood and Fire: The Attack on the King David Hotel* (New York: Putnam, 1981). Less gripping than Begin, but useful, is General George Grivas, *Guerrilla Warfare and EOKA's Struggle* (London: Longmans, 1964).

Religious terror

There is a consistently worthwhile collection of essays in Mark Juergensmeyer (ed.), *Violence and the Sacred in the Modern World* (London: Frank Cass, 1992), and a longer study of 'religious nationalism' by Juergensmeyer, *The New Cold War?* (Berkeley: University of California Press, 1993). Juergensmeyer's recent *Terrorism in the Mind of God* (Berkeley: University of California Press, 2000) engages with violence in three religious traditions, though it leaves hanging the question whether God is actor or audience in this terror process. There is a wide overview in Madawi al-Rasheed and Marat Shterin (eds.), *Dying for Faith: Religiously Motivated Violence in the Contemporary World* (London: Tauris, 2009). Jihadist thinking is lucidly addressed in Malise Ruthven, *A Fury for God:*

The Islamist Attack on America (London: Granta Books, 2002) and
Mary R. Habeck, *Knowing the Enemy: Jihadist Ideology and the
War on Terror* (New Haven and London: Yale University Press, 2006).
Fred Halliday offers a typically sharp essay on 'terrorisms in historical
perspective', in *Nation and Religion in the Middle East* (London:
Saqi Books, 2000). For a remarkable rethinking, see Faisal Devji,
*The Terrorist in Search of Humanity: Militant Islam and Global
Politics* (London: Hurst, 2008). Of five illuminating volumes on
fundamentalism by Martin E. Marty and R. Scott Appleby, see
especially *Fundamentalisms Comprehended* (Chicago: Chicago
University Press, 1995). Martin Kramer provides a forensic analysis
of Hezbollah in *The Moral Logic of Hizbullah* (Tel Aviv: Tel Aviv
University, 1987), and Ehud Sprinzak of Gush Emunim in *Brother
Against Brother* (New York: Free Press, 1999). There are several
interesting attempts to analyse suicide attacks, for instance Diego
Gambetta (ed.), *Making Sense of Suicide Missions* (Oxford: Oxford
University Press, 2005). There are contrasting interpretations in
Robert Pape, *Dying to Win: The Strategic Logic of Suicide Terror*
(New York: Random House, 2005) and Mia Bloom, *Dying to Kill:
The Allure of Suicide Terrorism* (New York: Columbia University Press,
2005). For the social networks, see Marc Sageman, *Leaderless Jihad*
(Philadelphia: Pennsylvania University Press, 2008).

Counterterrorism

John B. Wolf, *Antiterrorist Initiatives* (New York: Plenum Press,
1989) sets out the menu; Alex P. Schmid and Ronald D. Crelinsten
(eds.), *Western Responses to Terrorism* (London: Frank Cass, 1993)
collects a number of helpful essays on both regional and theoretical
issues. Benjamin Netanyahu (ed.), *Terrorism: How the West Can Win*
(London: Farrar, Straus, Giroux, 1986) is a famous right-wing call to
arms, whose loaded assumptions are loudly signalled in its title.
The call to abandon conventional restraints is amplified in Alan
Dershowitz, *Why Terrorism Works* (New Haven and London: Yale
University Press, 2002). There is a forensic examination of American
antiterrorist methods before 9/11 in John K. Cooley, *Unholy Wars:
Afghanistan, America and International Terrorism* (London: Pluto
Press, 1999), and a remarkable personal account in Richard A. Clarke,
Against All Enemies: Inside America's War on Terror (London: Simon
& Schuster, 2004). Later 'war on terror' strategy is assessed in Seth

Jones, *In the Graveyard of Empires: America's War in Afghanistan* (New York: Norton, 2009). Christopher Hewitt, *The Effectiveness of Anti-Terrorist Policies* (Langham, MD: University Press of America, 1984) is a rare attempt to find ways of measuring effects. For a pioneering example of 'critical terrorism studies', see Richard Jackson, *Writing the War on Terrorism: Language, Politics and Counter-Terrorism* (Manchester: Manchester University Press, 2005).

On the issue of democracy, Paul Wilkinson, *Terrorism Versus Democracy: The Liberal State Response* (London: Routledge, 2011) offers a commonsensical overview, though producing little evidence that terrorism threatens democracy as such. See also David A. Charters (ed.), *The Deadly Sin of Terrorism: Its Effect on Democracy and Civil Liberty in Six Countries* (Westport, Conn.: Greenwood Press, 1994). On the media in particular, see Alex P. Schmid and Janny de Graaf, *Violence as Communication: Insurgent Terrorism and the Western News Media* (Beverly Hills: Sage, 1982).

Index

Index

POLITICS
A Very Short Introduction
Kenneth Minogue

In this provocative but balanced essay, Kenneth Minogue discusses the development of politics from the ancient world to the twentieth century. He prompts us to consider why political systems evolve, how politics offers both power and order in our society, whether democracy is always a good thing, and what future politics may have in the twenty-first century.

'This is a fascinating book which sketches, in a very short space, one view of the nature of politics … the reader is challenged, provoked and stimulated by Minogue's trenchant views.'

Ian Davies, *Talking Politics*

'a dazzling but unpretentious display of great scholarship and humane reflection'

Neil O'Sullivan, University of Hull

www.oup.com/vsi

INTERNATIONAL RELATIONS
A Very Short Introduction
Paul Wilkinson

Of undoubtable relevance today, in a post-9-11 world of growing political tension and unease, this *Very Short Introduction* covers the topics essential to an understanding of modern international relations. Paul Wilkinson explains the theories and the practice that underlies the subject, and investigates issues ranging from foreign policy, arms control, and terrorism, to the environment and world poverty. He examines the role of organizations such as the United Nations and the European Union, as well as the influence of ethnic and religious movements and terrorist groups which also play a role in shaping the way states and governments interact. This up-to-date book is required reading for those seeking a new perspective to help untangle and decipher international events.

www.oup.com/vsi

ONLINE CATALOGUE

Very Short Introductions

Our online catalogue is designed to make it easy to find your ideal Very Short Introduction. View the entire collection by subject area, watch author videos, read sample chapters, and download reading guides.